imperial form

from achaemenid iran to augustan rome

● ● ● ellipsis

imperial form

from achaemenid iran to augustan rome

First published 1998 by
●●●ellipsis
55 Charlotte Road
London
EC2A 3QT
EMAIL ...@ellipsis.co.uk

ISBN 1 899858 40 7

Publisher Tom Neville
Designed by Jonathan Moberly
Edited by Vicky Wilson
Drawings by John Hewitt
Image processing by Heike Löwenstein
Glossary by Andrew Wyllie
Index by Diana LeCore
Printed and bound in Hong Kong

British Library Cataloguing in Publication Data: a catalogue
record for this publication is available from the British Library

contents

1 **Darius I in audience** relief from the so-called Treasury at Persepolis (Teheran, National Museum).

The age of empire, which culminated in the dominance of Rome, opened with the advent of Cyrus the Great (d. 529 BC) to power in Persia. His Achaemenid empire began with the conquest of Mesopotamia and Lydia. His son Cambyses invaded Egypt but died mysteriously soon afterwards, and the throne went to his cousin, Darius I (522–486 BC).[1] It was he who took the Persians across the Hellespont to Greece, where they were checked at Marathon in 490 BC, and where his son Xerxes I (486–466 BC) had finally to admit defeat at Salamis in 479 BC. (These victories gave the cities of Hellas the surge of pride and confidence that propelled them along the road to supreme cultural achievement and ultimately self-destruction, see volume 2, HELLENIC CLASSICISM.) One hundred and fifty years later, Darius III was defeated on his own ground by the Greeks under Alexander the Great of Macedon.[2]

The Persians had no monumental tradition of their own, religious or secular, but graduated to the need for one with the Achaemenid acquisition of imperial Babylon. Absorbing the former domain of the Hittites, Assyrian Urartu and even Egypt, they drew inspiration from all over their vast empire and transmitted it to

2 **The Battle of Issos** showing Alexander (far left) confronting Darius III (centre).
Mosaic pavement from the House of the Faun, Pompeii (Naples, Archaeological Museum).

their neighbours further east. Though they rose to prominence in an area which was dry and came to dominate a vast tract of western Asia notable for its deserts, they developed a monumental timber trabeated structural system – partly, no doubt, because they controlled the rich cedar forests of Lebanon. First, however, they were nomads living in tents – and in the many-poled marquees of the king's encampment lies the origin of the columned pavilions of the king's permanent establishment.

It was at Cyrus the Great's Pasargadae camp (see volume 1, ORIGINS, page 217) that the Persians seem first to have translated their informally distributed tents into multi-columned timber pavilions, drawing inspiration from the Urartians. Like them, they added columned porticos modelled on the Syrian bit-hilani. Seeking permanence and greater grandeur for the composite form – the apadana – in stone, Cyrus employed Ionian master masons. Then, in emulation of the great Assyrian palace platforms, of walled courts and rooms lined with orthostats and protected by lamassu, of the Babylonian equivalents with their glazed bricks, of the hypostyle halls of Egypt – not only sacred ones but also palatial ones like those of el-Malqata or Akhetaton (see volume 1, ORIGINS) – Darius I supplanted Pasargadae on a truly imperial scale at Susa and Persepolis, acknowledging his eclecticism in doing so.

The cult centre of Persepolis

Intended to eclipse Babylon, Susa was an administrative capital: much built over, most of it has been lost to unscientific excavation. Persepolis[3] was the dynastic cult centre devoted to the rites of the spring fertility festival: its remains are overwhelming. Beyond the

3 **Persepolis, Great Palace** begun c. 520 BC by Darius I and substantially completed a century later, plan and restored perspective from the north (OVERLEAF).

Entrance stairs (1) and propylaeum (2); apadanas of Darius I (3) and Xerxes I (4); triple gate tripylon (5), leading to the private apartments (hadith, meaning 'dwelling place') of Darius I (6), Xerxes I (7) and Artaxerxes III? (8); harem (9); offices (10).

Though emulating the Assyrians, the mountain-backed platform, 457 by 274 metres (1500 by 900 feet) and up to 18.3 metres (60 feet) high, has earlier Achaemenid precedents (notably at Pasargadae) which recall Urartian

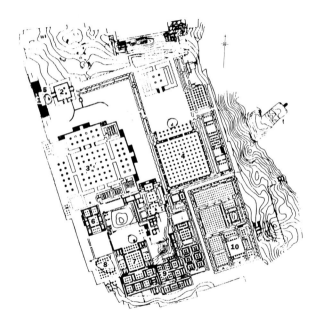

practice in their cyclopean masonry. The main elements,
though parallel to one another, are informally distributed
as at Pasargadae (see volume 1, ORIGINS, page 217) but
much closer together and usually square in plan.

On its own terrace, the apadana of Darius I was
76 metres (250 feet) square. It had a hall – 59 metres
(195 feet) square – of 36 stone columns, 2.1 by 18.3 metres
(7 by 60 feet), set 9.1 metres (30 feet) apart, a timber
coffered ceiling, lower bit-hilani porticos to the north, east
and west, and service rooms by the hadith to the south.
It was reached by two sets of broad stairs (north and east)

great ceremonial entrance,[4] guarded by syncretic monsters in the Assyrian (and Hittite) manner, the platform of the Great Palace was divided into three zones – as at el-Malqata and at oriental palaces down the ages from Mari and beyond (see volume 1, ORIGINS, pages 139 and 89). The outer zone was dominated by the apadanas in which the king held public audience.[6] A smaller, screened hall was provided for private audience in the central zone of the king's personal quarters (the hadith).[5] The innermost zone, the walled harem, alone recalls the typical Mesopotamian approach to palace design. The reliefs which represent

embellished with splendid tiered reliefs of Median and Persian soldiers and tribute-bearers from all over the empire. Xerxes 1's hall of 100 stone columns, with one portico to the north and corridors to the other three sides, was enclosed by screen walls. There were two doors in each wall, seven windows to the portico and seven niches in each of the other three sides. The hadiths also had one portico, but the central hall was flanked with living rooms. The first hall of the harem was similar: beyond it a grid of corridors served the royal women's individual apartments, most of which consisted of a square hall and two chambers.

4 **Persepolis, Great Palace, propylaeum** showing syncretic monsters.

Built under Xerxes I after the model of the one at Pasargadae, with syncretic monsters to both portals and a columned waiting hall between, this was the ceremonial entrance for official visitors – notably subject rulers.

5 **Persepolis, Great Palace, hadith of Darius I** view
from the east with the apadana of Darius I beyond.
   Spanned by Egyptian cavetto lintels and Ionic egg-and-
dart astragals, the niches and portals screening the private
audience hall – like those screening the apadana of Xerxes I
– were not assembled with distinct jambs and lintels, and
were sometimes even carved from a single block. Their sides
display reliefs of the king in appropriate modes.

6 Persepolis, Great Palace, apadana of Darius I view from the south.

7 Persepolis, Great Palace, apadana column reconstruction drawing.

Like the timber work, some of the columns were inlaid with precious metals and ivory. Most of them had slender fluted shafts in the Ionic manner. The Ionic torus, borrowed by Cyrus the Great from the great works of King Croesus of Lydia (560–546 BC), was supplemented at the base by a foliate bell-shaped moulding – though even this has later Ionic equivalents. The tassel-like fringe of drooping sepals at the base of the capital recalls the cord bound round the top of a timber post to prevent splitting: it has its equivalent in the Aeolic capital from Neandria and the proto-Ionic one from Naucratis, where the egg-and-dart ovolo is anticipated (see volume 2, HELLENIC CLASSICISM, pages 52–53). The corolla recalls the Egyptian palm-leaf motif (see volume 1, ORIGINS, page

62) and each segment is often etched with a papyrus flower. The scrolls of the block below the bracket recall Ionic volutes, doubled and disposed vertically as they sometimes were in the Levant and in Nebuchadnezzar's Babylon. The bracket with addorsed animals possibly derived from Urartu, but the Persians certainly made it their own.

The inscription celebrating the completion of the palace at Susa, which could equally well apply to Persepolis, begins: 'I am Darius, great king, king of kings, king of all lands, king of this earth… This is the palace I erected… From afar its ornamentation was brought… That the earth was dug down [to rock bottom], and that the rubble was packed down and that the brick was moulded, was due to the Babylonians.' After listing the far-flung origins of the stone and other precious materials, including cedar from Lebanon and ornamentation from Ionia, the king continues: 'The stone cutters who wrought the stone were Ionians and Sardians. The goldsmiths who wrought the gold were Medes and Egyptians… Those who wrought the baked brick were Babylonians. Those who adorned the wall were Medes and Egyptians…'

The synthesis achieved for Darius I was sustained virtually without change throughout 200 years of Achaemenid activity.

8 **Naqsh-i-Rustam** rock-cut tombs of Darius I (right) and ?Xerxes I.

the king and his entourage are Ionian in their elegance (see 1, page 6). The columns[7] are complex in their derivation, but while clearly indebted to Egypt, the designer of the capitals drew liberally (and irrationally) on the Ionic tradition and its sources.

Following the Median tradition of rock-cut tombs, Darius I and three of his successors had full-scale replicas of an apadana portico, complete with the dentillated cornice of a heavy beamed roof, carved into the cliff at Naqsh-i-Rustam for their burial.[8] The later Achaemenids reproduced the formula in the cliff behind Persepolis itself. Over the façades of their tombs and elsewhere the kings are depicted attending a ceremony at a fire altar under the protection of their great god, Ahura Mazda.[9] Standing sentinel before the royal necropolis at Naqsh-i-Rustam is a square tower usually identified as a fire temple.[10]

Achaemenid religion

Ahura Mazda presided over a family of deities brought to Iran by the Aryans – in much the same way as Zeus

9 **Persepolis, Great Palace, tripylon** the monarch and attendants under Ahura Mazda.

dominated the Greek pantheon. Like Indra in Vedic India, he was upholder of the good in the cosmic struggle against evil. As in Vedic India, too, religious ritual was centred on the sacrifice of a sacred juice (*haoma* in Iran, *soma* in India) at a fire altar. However, the officiating Mazdaist priests seem to have belonged to a clan (*magi*) rather than a caste.

Reformed before the advent of the Achaemenids by the semi-legendary Zarathustra (Zoroaster to the Greeks), the cult of Ahura Mazda anticipated monotheism. Aware of its god's supreme virtue, humanity is free to choose between good and evil but, at the final day of judgement, Ahura Mazda would preside over trial by fire in which the evil would perish. Ahura Mazda was thus the ideal model for Darius I and his successors as the Great King imposing order on earth.

10 Naqsh-i-Rustam, so-called Kaaba of Zardusht.

This Achaemenid single-room stone structure, 7.3 metres (24 feet) square and studded with blind windows, has variously been identified as a tomb, a treasury and a temple. The last explanation is thought most likely, with fire at its centre, but it is not clear how it was used.

The Achaemenids were tolerant of the religions of their subjects, however, and seem to have promoted syncretism. With the absorption of Assyria, Ahura Mazda took on the image of Ashur – or so it is generally assumed – though he was not originally conceived anthropomorphically. By the end of the 5th century BC, imperial experience of other traditions seems to have prompted the development of a triad, with the association of Ahura Mazda with Mithra (a sun-god like Indian Surya, if not Greek Apollo) and Anahita (a female deity like Ionian Artemis, though sometimes identified by the Greeks with Aphrodite and even Athena). Mithra seems to have been, or to have become, the specific dedicatee of *haoma,* though fire itself, specially sanctified as the essential element of purification, belonged to Ahura Mazda himself. The special status accorded to fire meant that cremation of the dead was proscribed, and the body was interred or, preferably, exposed for consumption by birds and animals.

Following the Peloponnesian Wars (431–371 BC), which destroyed the Hellenic commonwealth, pitting Dorians and Ionians against each other, Hellas came under Macedonian domination with the accession of Philip II in 359 BC, succeeded by his son Alexander in 336 BC. Alexander the Great not only sustained Macedonian dominance of Hellas, but led the Hellenes to overrun the Achaemenid empire, which by then extended to most of the world known to them. He died in 323 BC, and his vast domains were divided between his generals. The pragmatic Ptolemy Soter took Egypt, which he knew to be readily defensible, and assumed the mantle of pharaoh in 306. Alexander's governor of Babylon, Seleucos Nicator, took Syria and tried to hold sway over all the territories that had been incorporated into the main body of the empire, from the borders of India to the edge of Anatolia.

The Achaemenids had held the diversified peoples of west Asia together most effectively with their great army and firm grasp of administration – under the protection of Ahura Mazda and the inspiration of Mithra. But by the mid 4th century BC, in Ionia at least, their authority amounted to little more than

nominal hegemony over virtually independent monarchs. Though Alexander had settled colonies of vet-
eran soldiers throughout his conquered territories,
Seleucid control beyond what we now think of as
Syria, Palestine and eastern Turkey was even less
effective – despite their un-Hellenic assumption of the
religious aura which traditionally clothed kingship in
much of the area. The political problems of Alexander's successors are beyond our interest here, but the
devices of their theologians certainly concern us.

The cult of the ruler

In the world of the Greeks poised to conquer the
Achaemenids, the pantheon of Homer and Hesiod
which had held sway over the classical age of Hellenic
civilisation had been discredited by the catastrophe of
the Peloponnesian Wars. State honour sustained a
public role for the Olympian gods, but in private people looked elsewhere for solutions to ethical problems.
The aspiring dynast was naturally committed to see-
ing man in the image of the gods, but, turned about by
sophists like Protagoras ('Man is the measure of all
things'), gods in man's image had little to offer the
growing body of intellectuals committed to scientific

enquiry. Anthropomorphic mysticism was confronted
by anthropocentric rationalism. Yet as Hellenistic
monarchs could not fail to see, increasing numbers of
increasingly individualistic Hellenes were turning
from the emotional void left by the discrediting of Zeus
and his family to fate and foreign mystery cults promis-
ing personal salvation.

Attempts had been made to endow Zeus with a
sense of purpose as World Mind, and with morality
as Lord of Oaths, and he was now to be assimilated
to a variety of oriental creator-gods. In Egypt, most
significantly, Ptolemaic theologians furthered the
native syncretic tradition by identifying the Olympian
father with Amun-Re and his brother Hades with
Osiris – as whom Egyptian kings were always immor-
tal. Promoting a new royal cult, the new regime gave
the Graeco-Egyptian deity a new anthropomorphic
identity and associated the centre of his worship with
the greatest library of antiquity in the new capital,
Alexandria.

By the time of Ptolemy I, Osiris was especially
prominent in Lower Egypt in the circle of Ptah, the
old creator-god of Memphis. The cult was centred on
the compound at Saqqara where the progenitive Apis

bulls were kept in regulated succession, embalmed
and entombed. There – it is thought, not without
controversy – the soul of Osiris was believed to live
through the unbroken Apid line, and the mummified
animal was identified with him in worship as Osor-
Hapi. Ptolemy's theologians translated Osor-Hapi/
Hades into Serapis for their new Alexandrine cult.
Ptolemy's sculptors presented Serapis with a distinct
fraternal resemblance to Zeus, and the Romans were
to identify Serapis with Jupiter.[11]

As Osiris – son of the sun-god Re, the vegetation
god triumphant over death – Serapis promised salvation and naturally claimed the power of healing which
the Greeks ascribed to the sun-god Apollo, son of
Zeus. Just as naturally he claimed Osiris' wife and sister, Isis.[12] Her cult as healer was pre-eminent in Egypt
by the end of the dynastic period and embraced that
of Hathor, goddess of motherhood. Embarking with
Serapis on a new career, she in turn naturally claimed
the attributes of the sister of Zeus and Hades, Demeter – heiress of the great mother – and with them her
mysteries. After all, plants live again with her brother-
husband, whose resurrection was due to her
enchanted powers. Moreover, as the mother of Horus

through whom divinity came to earth in the pharaoh, Isis was also the mother of salvation. Mystic and pantheistic, indeed monotheistic in tendency, the cult was pregnant with promise for the future – here and in the life hereafter. Meanwhile, if Ptolemy became Osiris/Serapis in the afterlife, his queen became Isis. The great Serapeum disappeared with ancient Alexandria, but it is no accident that the best-preserved antique buildings in Egypt are Ptolemaic temples of Horus and Isis with royal birth houses.

The cult of the ruler was endemic in most of the world east of Hellas, and even in Hellas itself the post-Homeric tradition honoured men of exceptional achievement as comparable to the gods. What more natural in an anthropocentric state than that the king should claim such honours? Alexander seems to have become megalomaniac enough actually to believe in his own divinity. In Asia, as in Egypt, few of his successors went as far, but vulnerable as usurpers, they legitimised themselves with divine pedigrees (including blood relationship to Alexander in the case of Ptolemy). Vicars of god in life, their tangible omnipotence – earned in victory and through moral responsibility – promised more than their assumed ancestors

11 **Serapis** Roman bust,
c. AD 100 (Rome, Vatican
Museum).

Serapis bears a grain
measure (*modius*) on his
head as a symbol of his
Osirid powers of fertility.

12 **Isis** Graeco-Roman
bust, 2nd century AD
(Aghios Nikolaos, Crete,
Archaeological Museum.)

Isis bears the queen's
head-dress, including the
sun disc of her father and
the cow horns of Hathor.

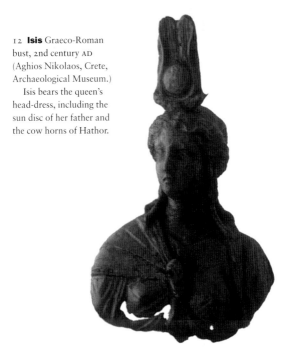

had realised, but not until they joined the line in death do they seem actually to have been worshipped.

Hellenistic monumentalism

The term 'Hellenistic' has been coined for the hybrid art forged from the cross-fertilisation of Hellenic and Asian ideals under Alexander and his heirs. The cultural consequences of the triumph of the Macedonians over the Achaemenids were profound, of course, but the influence of oriental attitudes on Ionia had been formative, and the importation of Greek ideals into Asia goes back at least to the founders of Pasargadae and Persepolis.

At the other end of the royal road – at Sardis, the former capital of Lydia from which the Persians ruled Ionia again after 387 BC when Artaxerxes II imposed his peace on the Hellenes to end the most recent bout in the Peloponnesian Wars – new prosperity recalled the age of King Croesus (560–546 BC) in lavish building, and eastern taste took liberties with convention. Palaces and civic amenities received more attention than in the golden age of the Hellenic polis, and so vast were the temples founded in Ionia at the time that most were beyond completion even after centuries of effort.

Conservative in planning, if sometimes free with the
Order, they emulated the Artemisium at Ephesus (see
volume 2, HELLENIC CLASSICISM, pages 60–61).

The great Temple of Apollo at Didyma,[13–14] where
much more remains than at Ephesus or Sardis, is perhaps the most spectacular example. With double porticos of ten columns (dipteral decastyle) the temple
remained unroofed, and a separate shrine sheltered the

13 OVERLEAF **Didyma, Temple of Apollo** begun c. 313 BC,
plan and reconstructed perspective view.

Built to the plans of Paeonius of Ephesus and Daphnis
of Miletus in replacement of an archaic temple destroyed
by Darius I in 494 BC, work dragged on for several hundred
years, but was left incomplete. With a stylobate of 51.1 by
109.3 metres (167 feet 9 inches by 358 feet 9 inches), it was
excelled in superficial area by the Artemisium at Ephesus
(see volume 2, HELLENIC CLASSICISM, pages 60–61) but by
few other Greek temples. Like the Artemisium, it was
dipteral but the outer pteron was unique in having ten by 21
columns set 5.3 metres (17 feet) apart. An antechamber was
inserted between the generous pronaos and elongated cella
and the opisthodomos was omitted. At 19.7 metres (64 feet
8 inches), the columns were not exceeded in height, and

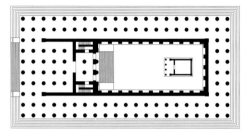

with proportions of 1:9.74 they are known to have been
surpassed in slenderness by no other significant Hellenic
work. The bases were exceptionally varied, most
conforming to the Asian norm with scotias and torus,
but several on the front had circular or polygonal blocks
instead. Several capitals (possibly executed under the
Attalids of Pergamon in the first half of the 2nd century BC
or even later under the Romans) had busts of gods or
animals entwined by the volutes. Medusa heads emerged
from the rich acanthus foliage of the frieze inserted (also
probably by the Attalids) in the entablature below the bold
dentils. The pediments were never executed and, despite the
massive proto-Ionic pilasters relieving its inner walls, the

cella was unroofed – indeed, it contained a grove of trees. Its floor, some 13 feet below the level of the antechamber and screened from it by piers with attached Corinthian columns, was reached from the north-east by a grand flight of steps on axis with a small prostyle hexastyle Ionic shrine housing the archaic statue of Apollo salvaged from the original temple. Of no specific Order, the broad capitals of the pilasters were linked by a continuous frieze.

14 Didyma, Temple of Apollo view from the north-east.

15 **Didyma, Temple of Apollo** cella interior from the south-west.

16 **Didyma, Temple of Apollo** interior pilaster capital.

17 **Athens, Choragic Monument of Lysicrates** 334 BC.

Among many types of commemorative or votive
monument erected in or on the way to sacred sites, trophies
won in choragic contests in the theatre were usually set up
on a pedestal in the sanctuary of Dionysius or in the street
leading to it. Superseding simple podia, in the 4th century
BC several of them took the form of miniature tholoi, most
notably the one erected by Lysicrates to display the trophy
he won in the contest of 334. Set on a square podium of
limestone and a circular stepped stylobate of blue marble,
the rotunda of white marble was ringed by six Corinthian
columns engaged to the cylindrical core. The capitals seem
overwrought, the acanthus leaves rising out of rushes, with
tendrils not growing naturally from them but improbably
joined into a heart-shaped form semi-detached from them.
For the first time in an external context, the Order was
given a full entablature with both sculpted frieze and dentils.

The precedent set here for the use of an attached
Order on the exterior of a building was not ignored by
Hellenistic builders. Perhaps the most notable example in
Hellas was the bouleterion of Miletus (see 39, page 86), where
the main building was like a pseudo-peripteral temple with
a podium-like basement supporting an engaged Order of
Doric columns all around the outside.

cult image at the head of the sunken inner court opposite the imposing flight of steps. The inner walls of the cella[15] are relieved with pilasters[16] conceived on a scale unprecedented except in the aberrant Temple of Olympian Zeus at Acragas (see volume 2, HELLENIC CLASSICISM, page 46).

Derived from the antae which had terminated portico walls from early archaic times, the buttress-like pilaster was to be the standard form adopted to limit the ambiguity implicit in confronting an Order with a wall. Applying Corinthian columns to the exterior of the Choragic Monument of Lysicrates in 334 BC,[17] the Athenians took the final step in exposing the structural pretensions of the Order as facile in that context. A tholos on a substantial podium, the Lysicrates Monument may be seen to descend from the same prototype as the Nereid Monument at Xanthus (c. 410 BC, see volume 2, HELLENIC CLASSICISM, page 146), in which a Lycian tradition seems to have been transformed by Athenians. The apotheosis of the form had been achieved by mid century in the Tomb of Mausolus of Halicarnassus[18] – the wonder of the world which gave its patron's name to the monumental tomb as a building type (mausoleum). Built to

18 OVERLEAF **Halicarnassus, Tomb of Mausolus
('Mausoleum')** 353 BC, reconstruction.

The site is now a hole in the ground and the building's
reconstruction on the basis of antique descriptions (by
Vitruvius and Pliny in particular) is still controversial. Pliny
divides the elevation into four parts: podium, peristyle,
pyramid and crowning statue group with a four-horse
chariot (*quadriga*). He gives the perimeter as 440 Ionic
feet (129.3 metres or 424 feet 5 inches), the total height
as 140 Ionic feet (41.1 metres or 135 feet), the height of
the pteron of 36 columns as 37.5 Ionic feet (11 metres or
36 feet 2 inches) and the height of the pyramid of 24 steps
as equal to that of the element below it – leaving the
remaining 65 Ionic feet (19.1 metres or 62 feet 8 inches)
to be divided between the podium and the *quadriga*
group (if the element below the pyramid is taken to be the
pteron alone). As Dinsmoor admirably reveals, the main
problems of reconstruction arise with the distribution of the
columns, the definition of the relative height of column and
entablature, the disposition of the three friezes, fragments
of which were recovered from the site, and the dimensions
of the base of the pyramid in relation to (and possible
support by) either the pteron or the cella.

However it is reconstructed, the Mausoleum – the work

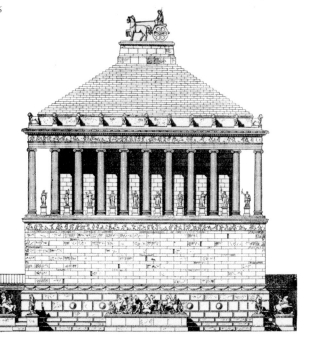

of Pythios and his sculptor Scopas (architect of the Temple
of Athena Alea at Tegea, see volume 2, HELLENIC
CLASSICISM, page 202) – represents the final permutation of
the Lycian tomb. With its temple-like structure on a high
podium, the Nereid Monument (see volume 2, HELLENIC
CLASSICISM, page 146) represents the penultimate phase late
in the 5th century BC, and a pyramid was added to the
formula for the so-called 'Lion Tomb' of Cnidus perhaps
early in the 4th century. But it was perfection of the formula
by Pythios and Scopas that earned the Mausoleum its
reputation and Mausolus the association of his name with
the monumental tomb forever.

Many rulers copied the Mausoleum at various scales.
The best surviving example, still with fragments of the
pyramid above its Corinthian colonnade, is the anonymous
tomb at Mylasa. Otherwise, various tomb types remained
popular in the Hellenistic period, including the tumulus, the
catacomb – with examples in Alexandria modelled on the
peristyle of a house – and the rock-cut temple front, as at
Telmessos, which was probably inspired by Achaemenid
practice (see 8, pages 20–21).

assert the pretensions of the former satrap of Caria, its reconstruction is controversial, though to the temple on its podium was certainly added the most potent image of royal immortality, the pyramid. The celebration of irresponsible might in the super-human size of the dynastic statues set between the columns, as in the conception of the whole, was characteristic of a civilisation whose faith in man had ceded to the realities of this world.

The Hellenistic canon

Pythios, the chief architect working for Mausolus at Halicarnassus, did more than anyone since the creation of the Artemisium at Ephesus (c. 356 BC, see volume 2, HELLENIC CLASSICISM, pages 60–61) to establish a canon for the Ionic Order. An account of the Tomb of Mausolus, which he wrote in collaboration with his principal colleagues, is now lost but his treatise on the Temple of Athena Polias at Priene,[19] begun c. 340 BC and dedicated to Alexander in 334, survives in fragments quoted by Vitruvius, and the standard was sustained by these.

   The west front of Pythios' temple was completed – or rebuilt – by Hermogenes of Priene just before the

19 OVERLEAF **Priene, Temple of Athena Polias**

c. 340 BC.

The temple had six by 11 columns of 1.3 by 11.4 metres
(4 feet 3 inches by 37 feet 6 inches), giving proportions of
1:8.84, on a base 19.5 by 37 metres (64 by 122 feet, a ratio
of 1:1.9). The rectangle defined by the columns' centres was
60 by 120 Ionic feet (17.6 by 35.2 metres or 58 by 116 feet).
The rectangle defined by the walls enclosing the cella,
elongated pronaos and truncated opisthodomos was 40 by
100 Ionic feet (11.75 by 29.38 metres or 38 feet 7 inches
by 96 feet 5 inches). Above square plinths, the bases of
the columns – 6 Ionic feet (1.76 metres or 5 feet 9 inches)
square and 6 apart, giving interaxial spacing of 12 Ionic
feet (3.5 metres or 11 feet 6 inches) – had a torus over
superimposed scotias as usual in Ionia. The volutes of the
capitals were joined by the traditional downward-curving
line, but the columns at the inner corners had contracted
whole volutes. As usual in Ionia, there were heavy dentils
but no frieze.

middle of the 2nd century BC. Hermogenes codified
the rules for Pythios' Order and based his own system
of ideal proportions on density, relating the diameter
and height of the column to the intercolumniation. Vitruvius drew heavily on Hermogenes, transmitting his
system to posterity, and quotes him as the source for
the statement that 'sacred buildings ought not to be
constructed of the Doric Order because faults and
incongruities were caused by the laws of its symmetry.' Doric was certainly still used for temples in the
Hellenistic period – alone, in combination with the
other Orders and in hybrid forms incorporating elements of the other Orders – but Ionic and Corinthian
buildings were far more numerous.

Urban planning: Priene

Pythios' temple dominated the grid of streets and
stepped alleys which enforced regular terracing on the
steeply contoured spur below Priene's high acropolis.[20–22] In the time-honoured way of the coloniser, the
imposition of a grid to discipline the rebuilding of dev-
astated cities or the development of new sites was common in the Hellenistic period. After the particular
approach credited to Hippodamus (see volume 2,

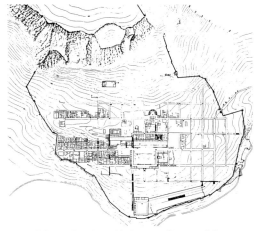

20 **Priene, site plan** with the acropolis top and the
palaestra bottom.

The grid of streets (east–west) and stepped alleys
(north–south) formed blocks of 120 by 160 Ionic feet
(35.4 by 47.2 metres or 116 by 155 feet) which enforced
regularity across, and largely against, the contours. The line
of the perimeter defences, by contrast, followed nature as
far as possible.

21 Priene
view of the site
from the west.

HELLENIC CLASSICISM, page 166) zones were defined by major arteries.

Public buildings were still not axially aligned within the grid, but both at Priene and within the originally organic growth pattern of Athens, the framing of ever-more extensive agoras with grand stoas was a regular feature. Sometimes of two storeys, these were often backed by shops or other public facilities, but their prime purpose was to provide a monumental context for civic dignitaries. Buttressed by the stoas lining the eastern entrance to the agora at Priene, the monumental arch first appears in Greek architecture extracted from its original context in defence walls.[23]

The central role in the grid at Priene is taken by the seat of the town's governing body, the discreet block of the ecclesiasterion.[24-25] Like the bouleterion (council chamber) of Athens, this had seats arranged on three sides of an altar in front of the speaker's platform. A prominent arch in the wall behind this platform was apparently original. Little is known about the roof: even between the intermediate columns, its span was wide, if not exceptional, and the reconstruction on the principle of the timber truss is controversial.

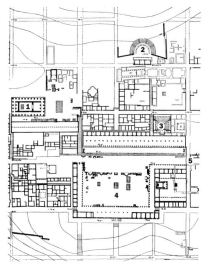

22 Priene, plan of the central area.

(1) Temple of Athena Polias; (2) theatre; (3) ecclesiasterion;
(4) agora, with its regular perimeter of stoas at the intersection
of the two main streets, and a secondary east–west artery
diverted behind the southern stoa; (5) monumental arch.

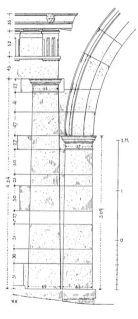

23 **Priene, monumental arch**

c. 150 BC.

Spanning the eastern entrance to the agora, the arch had a freestanding semi-circular Ionic architrave buttressed by the adjacent stoa walls.

24 **Priene, ecclesiasterion (house of assembly)**
view from the north.

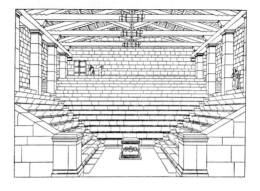

25 **Priene, ecclesiasterion** reconstructed interior and plan.

Within a rectangle 18.3 by 20.1 metres (60 by 66 feet) some 700 seats were arranged on three sides of an altar before the speaker's platform. This was covered by an arched vault, though the roof over the main space was carried on laminated timber trusses supported by columns later inserted behind the tiered seating. The seating was supported by the sloping ground. Entrance to the lower gallery, behind the speaker's platform, was from the level

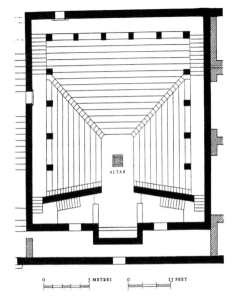

ALTAR

0   5 METRES   0   15 FEET

of the agora; entrance to the upper gallery, behind the top
row of seats, was from the street immediately below the
temple platform.

The theatre at Priene[26] is one of the earliest known to have had a stage building: the skene. This was the starting point for the development of the stage as we know it, with a backdrop for scenery rather than a view of the natural environment. Perhaps the most perfect surviving representative of the type is the contemporary theatre at Epidaurus.[27]

26 **Priene, theatre** c. 300 BC and later, view from the north-east.

In conformity with the example of the Theatre of Dionysius at Athens (see volume 2, HELLENIC CLASSICISM, page 151) – itself extended on a monumental scale in the mid 4th century BC and given a temporary stage towards the end of that century – the theatre at Priene marks the maturity of the type. Permanent timber stages seem first to have appeared at provincial centres – like Priene – possibly early in the 3rd century. The earliest stone ones were several generations later. The stage was usually raised on a Doric colonnade representing a palace – 2.7 metres (9 feet) high at Priene – and backed by a gallery (episcenia) which could be screened with scenery or used for interior sets.

Classical plays with limited action were probably performed in the orchestra (originally the dancing place),

against the background of the colonnade, while the raised stage was most plausibly designed to cater for complex modern plays. The city fathers would have sat in the semi-circle of chairs in the front row immediately before the orchestra.

27 PREVIOUS PAGES **Epidaurus, theatre** attributed by
Pausanias to Polycleitus the Younger and therefore
sometimes dated to the mid 4th century BC, but probably
built at the beginning of the 3rd century.

From the pure circle of the orchestra, 20.4 metres
(67 feet) in diameter, the auditorium's semi-circular banks
of seats fan out on a radius of 59 metres (193 feet 6 inches)
asserted by the stairways. There is a gangway at base level,
serving the special inner ring of seats for dignitaries, and
another somewhat more than half way up. Double the size
of Priene, the seating capacity was 12,000. As at Priene,
the only departure from true concentricity was the slight
splaying of the segments of seating beyond the base
diameter of the auditorium's semi-circle to limit the degree
to which they turn back upon the stage.

The original stage building seems to have contained a hall
– 19.5 by 6.1 metres (64 by 20 feet) – with parascenia
framing a narrow timber stage before it. The fully developed
stage, c. 300 BC, seems to have been raised on 14 piers with
attached Ionic half-columns 2.4 metres (8 feet) high. Access
to the raised stage was provided by ramps on each side.
Sometimes the permanent stage cut into the orchestra, but
here, as at Priene, it was built far enough back to preserve
a pure circle.

Hellenistic housing

Priene also provides important examples of 3rd-century BC houses.[28] The reconstruction of one excavated just to the west of the main temple – presumably a zone for the affluent – shows an entrance opening into a side passage which flanks the central court, preserving its privacy from the view of the street. The courtyard is roughly square, with the patron's megaron to the north and smaller rooms for the rest of the family and services on the other sides.

Most Hellenistic houses were built to similar plans,[29-31] though not necessarily with a clearly differentiated megaron. Light and air were drawn from the court and the outer walls were largely blind except where they were relieved by the occasional shop. Thus though regular, the streets of the domestic quarters were still little more than corridors for communication and drainage. Very different were the main arteries of the many new towns built or rebuilt to regular plans by Alexander and his Seleucid successors as bases for Hellenisation throughout their domains. Bordered by extended stoas, as at Apamea in Syria,[32] these were the most consistently magnificent streets the world had ever seen.

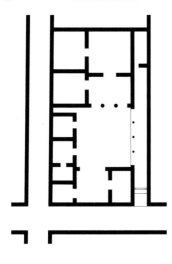

28 Priene, 3rd-century BC house plan.

The blocks in the more affluent quarters were divided into plots of 60 by 80 Ionic feet (17.6 by 23.5 metres or 58 by 77 feet), elongated north–south. Invariably four main rooms formed a block to the north of the court, so that the porch of the principal one (here a megaron) faced south over it. The entrance, always to the side and opening into a colonnaded passage, was from the north or south, according to the position of the plot in the block. The other sides of the court were bordered by the servants' quarters and storerooms. In the second century BC several houses at Priene, including this one, were renovated with a complete peristyle surrounding the court.

29 **Delos, 2nd-century BC house** plan.

The plots were irregular, as the town's development followed no formal plan, but in the typical house the rooms were ranged on three sides of a square Doric peristyle. There was usually a sunken trough (impluvium) in the centre of the peristyle and a rainwater cistern below fed from the roof through a pipe in one of the columns. Covered drainage channels led out to the extensive network of street drains.

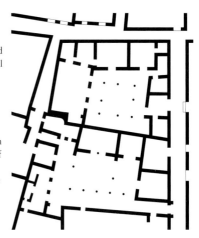

30 **Delos** view with courtyard houses in the foreground.

31 **Kos, house in the Hellenistic style** court with megaron portico and impluvium.

Pergamon and the Attalids

Occupied by Alexander, Caria was absorbed into the Seleucid empire along with most of Asia Minor – not without the opposition of the Ptolemies. In the late 260s BC the north-western province of Pergamon asserted its independence under its elderly governor's energetic nephew, Attalus I. Having repulsed an invasion of Celtic tribes (called Gauls) and defeated the Seleucids, Attalus went on to take Caria and proclaim

32 OVERLEAF **Apamea, main north–south arterial street.**

As in most of the towns laid out under Alexander and his successors, a grid of secondary streets framed rectangular blocks on either side of the main artery. Considerable variation was introduced to the type, with the location of the agora on or off the axis.

Though the ruined colonnades date mainly from a later period, they derive from the extension of the Hellenistic stoa. The street with continuous colonnades imposed on the fronts of its individual buildings seems to have originated in Syrian towns like Apamea early in the 1st century AD. It had reached east to Palmyra by the end of that century and west to the Aegean coast of Asia Minor shortly afterwards.

himself king over most of Ionia. His dynasty dominated the area until the last of his line bequeathed his kingdom to the Romans in 133 BC.

Possibly inspired by Halicarnassus – which Vitruvius admired as 'theatrical' – the Attalids exploited the natural contours of a splendid site in developing their seat at Pergamon.[33-35] The acropolis – among the most magnificent in the whole of antiquity and a text-book example of Greek planning – was crowned by a series of terraces containing the major public and cult buildings. The terraces fan out as they ascend the curved hill around the theatre, whose orchestra draws the composition together. The way the terraces are related to one another is no less significant. The middle one, at least, was carried on arcades of a monumentality unprecedented in Greek architecture.

The defeat of the barbarian Gauls was celebrated in the Great Altar erected to Zeus on the first of the terraces.[36] The altar is nearly square, but it is not set in a square compound and its back is out of alignment with the entrance wall. The view through the columns of the propylaeum is aimed not at the centre of the frieze embellishing the base of the altar, but just to the left of the

33 **Pergamon, acropolis** developed under Attalus I and
Eumenes II (whose reigns spanned from 241 to 159 BC),
view from Asclepion.

34 **Pergamon, acropolis** model (Berlin, Pergamon
Museum).

35 Pergamon, acropolis
plan.

(1) Lower terrace with
Great Altar of Zeus; (2) middle
terrace with Temple of
Athena Polias and its precinct;
(3) upper terrace with the
Temple of Trajan on the site
of the main Attalid palace;
(4) barracks; (5) grand peristyle
houses for principal members
of the royal entourage;
(6) citadel gate; (7) Heroum,
the palatial shrine of the deified
kings; (8) agora; (9) Theatre
and sanctuary of Dionysius.

The residential quarters
were ranged down the southern
slope of the hill towards the
main agora and sanctuary of
Demeter. Further settlement
was associated with a
sanctuary of Asclepius on
the plain below.

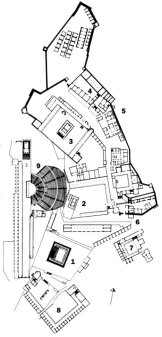

36 **Pergamon, acropolis, Great Altar of Zeus** view of
the north wing.

Commissioned by Eumenes II (197–159 BC) to
commemorate Attalid victory over the Gauls, this work on
the lower terrace of the Pergamene acropolis took the most
ancient of Hellenic building types to its apotheosis. The
traditional Hellenic altar was a narrow pedestal equal in
width to the temple associated with it. Here, the Great Altar
stood in its own precinct on a podium 36.4 by 34.2 metres
(119 feet 6 inches by 112 feet 3 inches) and 5.3 metres (17
feet 6 inches) high, approached from the west and walled to
the north, east and south. An Ionic colonnade to the outside
of the wall and piers with attached Ionic columns to the
inside both continued across the west front. A frieze in
low relief, depicting the Pergamene foundation myth,
embellished the inside of the wall. The great frieze – 2.3
metres (7 feet 6 inches) high – representing the battle of gods
and giants in high relief ran all around the podium, except
where the broad flight of steps ascended to the altar terrace.

Hermogenes of Priene imitated this work on a smaller
scale while renovating Pythios' Temple of Athena Polias
at Priene and as an integral part of his own scheme for
the Temple of Artemis Leucophryene at Magnesia-on-
Menander.

right-hand corner. The narrative related by the frieze –
the dynastic struggle against the Gauls represented as
the struggle between gods and giants – begins and, after
circumscribing the building, culminates here.

Viewed from the centre of the portico, the altar's
right-hand corner and the end of the building above
the right-hand side of the precinct frame the principal
dynastic cult temple dedicated to Athena up on the
next terrace. On the top terrace, the site of the
Attalid palace, the informal relationship of spaces in
accordance with sight lines, so characteristic of the
Greeks, was superseded by the rigorous symmetry of
the Temple of Trajan – but that was the work of
the Romans.

The role of the Orders

Dating from c. 250 BC, the Temple of Athena Polias
was Doric. Even in combination with Ionic proportions, this was exceptional among Hellenistic temples.
But Doric was often used for stoas like the ones framing the precinct here and those of the Athenian agora,
where the Pergamene formula was repeated (see volume 2, HELLENIC CLASSICISM, page 162). The main
one to the north of the temple platform here, before

the celebrated library, had two storeys, Doric below and Ionic above.[37]

The superimposition of the Ionic over the weightier Doric was to be canonical for multi-storey buildings. But the Ionic Order of the Pergamene stoa had a Doric frieze – an uncanonical hybrid style not atypical of the Hellenistic era. The Palace of Ptolemy III at Ptolemais,[38] for instance, had an external Order of engaged Ionic columns with a Doric frieze. The bouleterion at Miletus,[39] commissioned by Antiochus IV of Syria (175–164 BC), had Doric pilasters with freestanding Ionic columns inside and Doric half-columns outside.

Ionic was by far the most popular Order among Hellenistic patrons – even in Egypt where the Ptolemies usually sustained the ancient Egyptian tradition, except in domestic buildings and tombs imitating domestic buildings. But the Corinthian cause was furthered by the Seleucid kings from their advent at the end of the 4th century BC. In commissioning the completion of the great Athenian Temple of Olympian Zeus,[40] it was above all Antiochus IV who promoted Corinthian to a major role (see volume 2, HELLENIC CLASSICISM, page 205). Complete columns from his

37 Pergamon, precinct of Athena, stoa restored elevation with mixed Doric and Ionic Orders on the first-floor gallery.

On the great arcaded central terrace built before the middle of the 2nd century BC, the Doric Temple of Athena Polias had a stylobate 12.3 by 21.8 metres (40 feet 3 inches by 71 feet 5 inches) supporting six by ten columns 0.76 by 5.26 metres (2 feet 6 inches by 17 feet 3 inches), a ratio of 1:6.98.

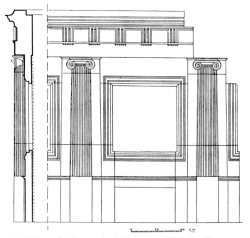

38 **Ptolemais (Cyrenaica), Palace of Ptolemy III**
part elevation.

39 **Miletus, bouleterion (council chamber)** c. 170 BC,
section and reconstructed perspective.

40 OVERLEAF **Athens, Temple of Olympian Zeus** founded
by the heirs of Peisistratos c. 520 BC, re-begun under
Antiochus IV in 174 BC to the design of Cossutius (a Roman
citizen probably of Greek origin), completed and dedicated
under Hadrian in AD 132.

On a stylobate 41.11 by 107.9 metres (135 by 354 feet),
a ratio of 1:2.62, were eight by 20 columns 1.93 by
16.9 metres (6 feet 4 inches by 55 feet 5 inches), giving
proportions of 1:8.81, in the outer pteron, and six by 18
columns in the inner pteron. The pronaos was walled (with
no columns in antis) and balanced to the east of the cella
by an adytum in place of an opisthodomos. According to
Vitruvius, the cella was unroofed, and it is probable that the
columns originally designed to support a roof were those
taken to Rome by Sulla in 86 BC to be incorporated in the
rehabilitation of the Temple of Jupiter Capitolinus.

Cossutius' design for the Corinthian capitals marks the
full maturity of the type, with the proportions of those in
the tholos in the sanctuary of Asclepius in Epidaurus
(c. 360 BC) combined with the caulicolus introduced at the
Temple of Athena Alea at Tegea (c. 350 BC). Here, spiral
fronds curved to the sides and the centre, as at Epidaurus,
and each pair sprung from a single caulicolus out of higher
acanthus leaves than at Tegea.

41 **Athens, Tower of the Winds** c. 48 BC, probably
initiating work on the new agora commissioned by Julius
Caesar at that time.

Attributed to Andronicus Cyrrhestes, the marble octagon
some 7.9 metres (26 feet) in diameter and 14.3 metres (47

unfinished work were transported to Rome and were
to prove formative of Roman taste. But in return, the
Romans gave much to Greece, Athens in particular –
most notably a new agora incorporating the celebrated
Tower of the Winds.[41]

feet) high was entered through two Corinthian porticos and
contained a water clock. The frieze at the top represented
each of the winds from the points of the compass addressed
by the sides. The weather-vane, turned by the wind to point
to the appropriate relief with his staff, was a bronze Triton
pivoted on a Corinthian capital at the apex.

   Towers were by no means uncommon in the Hellenic and
Hellenistic eras: defence works incorporated innumerable
examples. But it was the Pharos of Alexandria, built for
Ptolemy II (285–246 BC) by Sostratus of Cnidus to a height
of 134 metres (440 feet), that raised the category to the scale
of the wonders of the world.

42 **Jacques Louis David: 'Oath of the Horatii'** 1784
(Paris, Louvre).

According to tradition, Rome was founded in 753 BC. History is slightly different, but certainly 1000 years later, still 200 years before her fall, Rome was the greatest city and the capital of the greatest empire the world had ever seen. By the end of the 1st millennium BC she had changed out of all recognition[43–44] and her authority wavered, but there was to hand in the Emperor Augustus (27 BC–AD 14) a remarkable man to set it on a new course – if in a familiar guise. Rome's empire and her architecture were to be emulated for most of the centuries to come by all who would be grand.

Though Minoan and Mycenaean traders reached southern Italy towards the middle of the 2nd millennium BC, they seem to have made no impression on the primitive indigenous pastoralists, who have left little more than the traces of conical huts. Aryan tribes must have been infiltrating the area at much the same time: their Appenine settlements, including Rome, were distinguished by large rectilinear houses, and many of them were stoutly fortified by the end of the millennium. Their culture was transformed with the introduction of iron, perhaps by a final wave of invaders, and as a result they were able to extend their sway over

43 **Rome c. 300 BC** view to the north (model in the
Museum of Roman Civilisation, Rome).

Of the site's seven hills, the Aventine rises to the south-
west (bottom left here); to its north-east, beyond the Circus
Maximus, is the Palatine; to the north-north-west of that
is the Capitoline, dominating the Forum Boarium by the
bend in the river (towards the top left here) and the Forum
Romanum (centre); beyond this the Quirinal, Viminal and
Esquiline range from north to east (top right); and the
Caelian rises towards the south-east (bottom right).

44 **Rome c. AD 330** view to the north over the Circus
Maximus and Palatine (model in the Museum of Roman
Civilisation, Rome).

much of Italy – both as soldiers and as farmers. Their new hilltop villages, founded as centres for mining and improved farming, included major ones on the Palatine and neighbouring hills. The urban complex of Rome began when these were united in the 7th century BC about the low central plain which was to be their common forum. The houses were of wattle and daub, like the Appenine ones, and they were built to standard rectangular plans, though no regularity of village planning is evident.

Rome's rise to power

Well before the unification of Rome, two energetic new peoples had entered the scene. Attracted by the fertile plains and plentiful supplies of minerals – and preceded by Phoenicians with ideas from the near east – archaic Greek colonists brought a virile culture, already relatively well developed. They reached as far north as Cumae, just over 200 kilometres (125 miles) south of Rome. To the north of Rome, between the Tiber and the Arno, were the Etruscans. Ancient tradition identifies them as immigrants from Asia Minor, in particular Lydia, but the lack of recognisable linguistic links with the peoples there has suggested to some scholars that they emerged from the indigenous peoples. If so, they were clearly impressed by their Aryan invaders and adopted and developed their culture a century before their neighbours did.

The Etruscans maintained independent city states, inspired by the Hellenic polis, for 500 years from the late 7th century BC. Their constitutions varied and they squabbled over territory and trade, but they formed a loose confederation which controlled all Italy from the Po to Campania for over 100 years. Latium was included, and the Etruscans seem to have had a formative influence on the religion, constitution and fabric of the towns which were to become Rome.

The Etruscans lost Latium with the expulsion of the Tarquin kings and the establishment of a republic by the Romans in 509 BC. Capua, the Etruscan confederation's capital, was lost to the Samnites about 423, and with it went Campania. Pressing up from the south, the Romans took their first major Etrurian prize in 396. Meanwhile, the Gauls had begun harassing the Etruscans from the north in the 5th century BC, took the Po valley c. 400 and went on to sack Rome in 386. The Etruscans presented protracted resistance and defensive walls[45] to both sets of invaders, but by the end

45 Perugia, walls and so-called Gate of Augustus
c. 300 BC.

The Etruscans defended their towns by supplementing the natural escarpments of their elevated sites with great ashlar walls. The Romans learned to do the same – though the Servian Wall, which unified the defences of the settlements on the seven hills, was of stone-faced earthworks. This was consolidated largely after the settlements' primitive individual defences, which reinforced

of the 4th century BC – the Gauls having been subdued
and Latium dominated in the process – Rome had won
supremacy over most members of the confederation
and was in direct contact with the Greeks in the south.
By the middle of the next century, she had extended a
system of alliances across Samnite Campania to all
Magna Graecia.

On this basis Rome was able to challenge Carthage,
the main power in the western Mediterranean, im-
planted by Phoenician maritime adventurers in north
Africa and extending to Spain, Sicily, Sardinia and
Corsica. After the loss of these three great islands in
the 240s BC, and epic retaliation in which African and
Spanish forces were led by Hannibal to the very gates

cliffs with terraced walls and crossed flatter ground with
dykes and ditches, had been overcome by the Gauls c. 386.

The Greeks of Campania recognised the strength and
ceremonial value of the voussoir arch in defensive works
at least as early as the 5th century BC at Velia and Paestum
(see volume 2, HELLENIC CLASSICISM, page 177). In the
earliest Etruscan arches the voussoirs did not match the
courses, but they were being cut to fit by the 4th century,
when the earliest-known Roman examples appear.

of Rome, the Carthaginians were beaten in 202 and
Spain annexed. Finally, attempting resurgence,
Carthage itself was destroyed in 146 BC and Rome
annexed north Africa. She was then free to turn her
attention to the east.

Numen: god of ulterior purpose

In his *Oath of the Horatii* (see 42, page 92), the late 18th-
century French painter David shows the sons of
Horace swearing on their swords not to return from
war unless victorious, to live only to honour their family and to serve the state. Promoting the revival of
moral rigour in its own time, the painting admirably
represents the austere discipline of the early Romans
in their essentially religious dedication to a superior
purpose.

Ulterior purpose, the motive force behind all exis-
tence – comparable with fate – was deified as Numen
in central Italy. Knowing, as farmers and soldiers,
that man could not hope to deflect the inexorable from
its predetermined course, the Romans sought to
co-operate with it – like their Etruscan mentors.
Beyond the lessons of practical experience, this
depended on the ability of special diviners (augurs) to

determine Numen's purpose through the interpretation of omens (auspices) discernible in certain natural phenomena – in particular the conformation of sacred birds in flight over sanctified ground reflecting the ritual quartering of the sky and the configuration of the similarly quartered entrails of sacrificial animals. The formulas for the rites of augury and the design of its precincts passed to the Romans from the Etruscans. So too did the anthropomorphic conception of Numen's named manifestations (numina) as deities, which the Etruscans derived from the Greeks. Jupiter, the power of the sky (Zeus), was first, but he was soon joined as father in a family triad by Juno, the mother (Hera), and Minerva, wisdom (Athena).

The political system

Highly authoritarian beliefs promoted a highly authoritarian society. It was dominated by the father, who had the power of life and death over the members of his family. He was responsible for propitiating Numen and was thus a priest. The king was high priest but the fathers formed colleges to assist him in regulating religious practice, in reading the auspices and in tending particular manifestations of Numen.

The king was appointed by a council of senior patriarchs (the senate) on the approbation of the people. Following the rejection of the autocratic pretensions of the Tarquin kings in 509 BC, the senate and the people appointed two consuls to share the power of the king (imperium). The consuls were replaced each year, but could be superseded by a sole dictator for a strictly limited period in times of crisis. Since the senate met regularly, unlike the council of the people, and the consuls were checked by each other (and their short term of office), the senior patriarchs and their families (patricians) predominated. To counter this, the majority of the populace (plebeians), who manned the army and increased as trade grew with the empire, first won the right for their council to appoint protectors (tribunes), then under certain circumstances to pass statutory resolutions (plebiscites), and finally to promote a plebeian to one consulship each year. Further extension of popular rule was checked by the protracted wars with Carthage. These promoted the power of the executive and the strength of the senate, into which all ex-magistrates were automatically enrolled, increasing its representativeness and authority.

Early Roman architecture

Submission to authority was central to Roman republican mores, and the severe discipline of structure characterises early Roman building. Like the ashlar walls and voussoir arches of Perugia (see 45, page 98), this was the legacy of the Etruscans, who may have brought their skills to Italy from Anatolia, but probably derived the arch from the Greeks in Campania. Adept at supplementing the natural defences of hill and river with walls built against Gauls and Etruscans, and pre-eminent at engineering, the pragmatic Romans for a long time left art to the Etruscans and Campanian Greeks, from whom the Etruscans themselves had derived the simple, robust Order with which they disciplined their native tradition. And if the Romans depended on imported architects, their conception of both temple and house was also a response to the beliefs they shared with the Etruscans.

Etruscan houses and tombs

From the 6th century BC most urban Etruscans lived in modest rectangular houses in regularly planned towns, apparently reproduced in their necropolises,[47]

46 **Cerveteri (Caere), Banditaccia cemetery** 7th–3rd
century BC, view over the necropolis showing tumuli.

47 **Cerveteri, Banditaccia cemetery** view over the
necropolis showing streets of imitation houses.

48 Cerveteri, Banditaccia cemetery part plan showing tumuli and excavated square and megaron tombs.

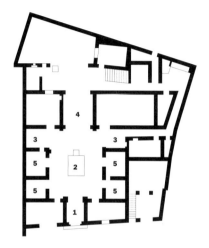

49 **Pompeii, 'Surgeon's House'** c. 300 BC, plan.
(1) Entrance hall (vestibulum); (2) atrium (with
impluvium inserted later); (3) transept wings (alae);
(4) principal room (tablinum) used as master bedroom;
(5) bedrooms (cubiculae).

where, earlier, even the primitive burial mounds (tumuli) were regularly arranged.[46] Looking back at the Etruscan record after several centuries of affluence and expansion, Vitruvius lists seven house types, though in fact these can be reduced to two: several rectangular rooms aligned along a single axis, like the megaron;[48] or a variety of rooms arranged around a relatively expansive nuclear space (atrium) with the principal room (tablinum) occupying most of the side opposite the entrance.[49] The former is common among the remains of early Etruscan settlements; the latter has so far been found first in the Samnite south from the beginning of the 3rd century BC. The atrium type was later extended with a colonnaded court (peristyle) – borrowed from the Greeks – to provide a more private nuclear space beyond the tablinum.

Houses were reproduced more or less to full scale as rock-cut tombs from the 7th century BC, and in miniature as terracotta models for the interment of the deceased's ashes from about 400.[50] Within the primitive form of the tumulus, the earlier tombs follow the form of the megaron, but with an inclined access passage instead of a porch. This type occasionally had a pitched roof expressed as a gable on the entrance front

50 **Funerary urn** 3rd century BC.
The urn reproduces in miniature a gabled house with an
arched entrance (Florence, Archaeological Museum).

51 **Cerveteri, Banditaccia cemetery, Tomba della Capanna (Hut)** late 7th century BC.
A primitive megaron with a pitched roof.

52 Cerveteri, Banditaccia cemetery, Tomba della Casetta (Little House) 6th century BC.
A developed megaron with slightly pitched ceilings over successive rectangular rooms.

53 Cerveteri, Banditaccia cemetery, Tomba dei Rilievi (Reliefs) late 4th century BC, early atrium type.

Etruscan house tombs often have sumptuous Orders – usually Aeolic, Ionic or Corinthian – and reproduce the joinery of ceilings, doors and windows. Red dados trimmed with a wave moulding are common, and many had frescoes depicting scenes from everyday life or heraldic devices. The latter occasionally appear in low relief, as in the Tomb of the Reliefs, perhaps the most elaborate Etruscan house tomb and reflected in the ceiling of the main hall,[51] though usually a succession of rectangular rooms had only slightly pitched ceilings.[52] The more lavish, later tombs have an increasingly large central space corresponding to the atrium, with a main room like the tablinum on axis with the entrance and several smaller chambers to the sides.[53] The atrium roof often had a central opening (compluvium) and was sometimes supported by four columns. It could be flat or slope down or up from the sides to the centre (impluviate or displuviate respectively).[54] These alternatives account for the sub-types listed by Vitruvius; the impluviate

extant. Its single chamber, excavated from tufa below ground level and without the tumulus usual at the site, has 13 double burial niches in the walls and some 30 compartments on the floor. The pair of rectangular piers supporting the slightly pitched roof have Aeolic motifs in their capitals. The low-relief stucco work represents arms, tools and domestic utensils as hanging on the walls. Each niche has a pair of tufa-cut beds and cushions. To the base of the parapet below the main one, on axis with the entrance, is a low bench with a pair of sculpted sandals. To its left is a chest with folded clothing.

54 **Tarquinia, Tomba di Mercareccia** 3rd century BC.
An example of the relatively rare displuviate atrium
type tomb.

variety was common among the remains of towns later developed by the Romans.

The temple

The religion of the Etruscans seems first to have focused on rites of augury performed in a ritually quartered, sanctified enclosure (templum). The addition of a monumental building followed contact with the Greeks. This was a megaron in essence, but unlike the Greek temple it stood on a podium with a single flight of steps to the front, and addressed the sanctified ground before it – as the tablinum addressed the atrium in the house – with a single portico, as in the Belvedere Temple at Orvieto.[55-56] This provided a stage for the performance of the augurs under the auspices of the deity in the cella. The pronaos columns were occasionally continued along the sides of the cella, but not the back, and the portico always stood free in distinction from the rest, as in the great Roman Temple on the Capitoline with its triad of cellas dedicated to Jupiter, Juno and Minerva.[57] Thus service to the authority of Numen is acknowledged in the authority of the axis and in the hierarchical disposition of the elements along it from the entrance to the cult

55 **Orvieto, Belvedere Temple** 5th century BC, view of the remains from the south-west.

56 **Orvieto, Belvedere Temple** plan and elevation.

Typically, a square precinct (temenos) with freestanding altars was entered at the centre of its southern side, opposite the steps and portico of the shrine building (contrary to the Greek norm of east–west orientation, recommended by Vitruvius).

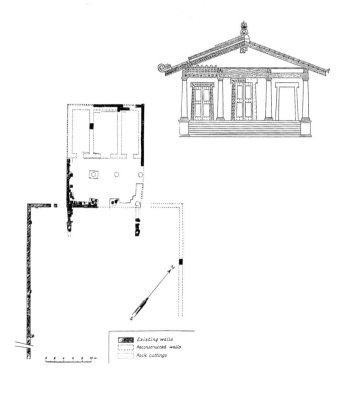

Existing walls
Reconstructed walls
Rock cuttings

0 2 4 6 8 10m

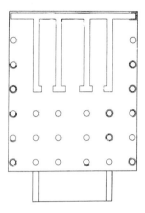

57 **Rome, Temple of Jupiter Capitolinus** plan of
Etruscan foundation attributed to Tarquinius Priscus
(616–579 BC), completed under Tarquinius Superbus
(535–509 BC), and dedicated in 509.

Originally of timber, brick and stucco on a stone base
62.25 by 53.3 metres (204 by 174 feet), the temple burned
down in 83 BC and was rebuilt to the old plan in marble
with columns from the Athenian Temple of Olympian Zeus.
It was rededicated in 69 BC.

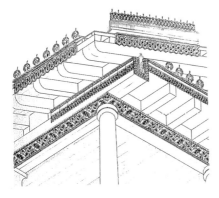

58 Cosa, Capitolium reconstructed detail of the portico showing the decorative terracotta revetment.

Typically, the rafters continued well beyond the line of the architrave to provide the eaves, and the longitudinal joists projected to the front, supporting a subsidiary roof below the pediment. The design of much of the detail derived from archaic Greek practice, though the Italians were more capricious than their mentors in the conception of fabulous form.

59 **Sovana, so-called Tomba Idelbranda** 2nd century BC.
Imitating a hexastyle temple with a triple cella and three
columns returning on each side (like the Roman Temple of
Jupiter Capitolinus but without the deep portico), this late
Etruscan, Hellenised rock-cut work incorporates a burial
chamber below its podium.

image standing before the blind back wall of the cella.

The column was usually an unfluted version of the Doric with echinus and abacus, and there is invariably a simple torus base derived from the Ionic. The four columns of the typical Etruscan portico are widely spaced. Architraves were made of timber long after masonry was introduced for columns in the 6th century BC, and the timber structure of the roof permitted wide eaves for the protection of the mud-brick and timber walls of the cella. The exposed timber, in turn, was protected by a richly moulded terracotta revetment.[58] The podium was built of stone from early in the 7th century BC, soon after the introduction of the rock-cut tomb.[59]

The authority of the plan

The regular geometry and axial alignment of the elements of the Etruscan temple complex provided a nucleus of urban order. In the early hill villages, the norm was organic growth, governed by the contours of the site and defined by the lines of defence. Formality, preserved in necropolises, appears in new settlements founded on the plains after expansion into Campania brought the Etruscans into contact with the

Greek colonists. There is evidence for orthogonal planning in Magna Graecia from at least as early as the mid 6th century BC, and the Etruscans must have been impressed by its efficiency. The first traces of an Etruscan town grid are at Marzabotto near Bologna.[60]

The Romans of the late republic believed they had learned land surveying from the Etruscans. There is no evidence that the Etruscans had developed it before their contact with the Greeks. Herodotus thought the Greeks had derived it from Egypt, where its institution by the pharaoh made it a sacred science – but the Greeks probably adopted it pragmatically. In Etruria, though obviously practical and somewhat irregular, it shadows the ritual quartering of the sky. In Etruria and Rome, as in Egypt, the forging of temple complexes from interdependent parts aligned axially – providing

60 **Marzabotto** founded in the late 6th century BC and destroyed by the Gauls in the early 4th century, plan.
    The town was strictly oriented by surveyors – flat stones at major intersections have been identified as the base for the *groma* (the principal implement of the ancient surveyor, consisting of a horizontal cross on a vertical staff for sighting the grid lines). The rectangular blocks, defined by

three main east–west arteries and one running north–south,
varied in width but were consistent in length. Etruscan
cemeteries laid out on a grid, seeming to reproduce the
houses and streets of a town, precede Marzabotto by at least
a generation.

a nucleus of order even in the unplanned town – contrasts with the discretion preserved for their entities by both the Dorians and Ionians.

The foundation of Rome, of course, long predates town planning. Even after being sacked by the Gauls in 386 BC, the city was rebuilt with primitive irregularity following the contours of the site. The low-lying land between the hills was prey to flood, and fire became an even worse hazard as people crammed in from all over the expanding empire. However, regularity was the hallmark of the fortified colonies of Roman citizens established to control the expanding network of the republic's dependencies all over Italy. With the extension of Rome's power beyond Italy, the pattern was repeated all around the Mediterranean – especially in the west, where the town was the novel vehicle of civilisation. Surprisingly enough, it was at the outset of this process, in conflict with Epirus c. 275 BC, that the Roman army learned the advantage of formal organisation in its camps. Thereafter the order of town and camp conformed – and nowhere closer than at Timgad and the camp of Lambaesis from which it was founded at the close of the 2nd century BC.[61-62]

The authoritarian approach to planning for an

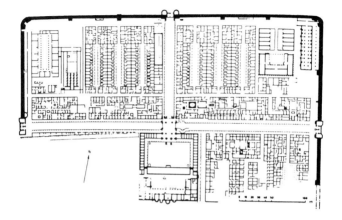

61 **Lambaesis** end of 2nd century BC, camp of the Third
Legion protecting the frontiers of the provinces of Africa
and Numidia (in modern Algeria), plan.

Facilitating the efficient deployment of the garrisons,
the two main axes and a complete circuit of streets within
the walls framed the grid of lanes which regimented the
disposition of houses or tents in the quarters.

62 **Timgad (Thamugadi)** 100 BC, colonial town founded
for veterans of the Third Legion, plan.

Within a century the colony had outgrown the original
square settlement with its rigid grid laid out by the military
engineers from nearby Lambaesis, and had expanded along
the external arteries.

The ideal unit was the square of 2400 Roman feet,
equalling 100 smallholdings (hence *centuratio*), oriented
to the cardinal points. Of course, practice was generally
determined by the condition of sites chosen for their
defensive potential (at first) or their administrative or
commercial advantages. The regularity of Timgad was
therefore exceptional. Theoretically centuriation of territory
was independent of town planning, but it was often
convenient for the two to converge, and certainly for the
rural decumanus (and even the cardo) to continue as the
main town arteries (though these names are not applied to
them with ancient authority). The principle came nearest
to realisation on the plains of northern Italy along the
Via Aemilia.

Frontinus (*Strategemata* IV,1,14) maintains that the
Romans learned the advantages of formal encampment after
overrunning the camp of Pyrrhus of Epirus in 275 BC.
Pyrrhus had crossed the southern Adriatic to Italy from his

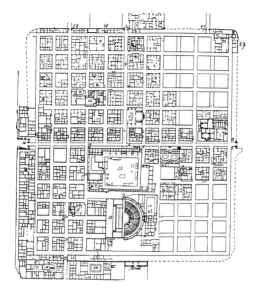

kingdom north-west of Greece in response to the appeal from Thurii for aid against Rome. Varro (*Antiquities*, 47 BC) traces the origin of the Roman *limites* back to Etruscan lore (*disciplina Etrusca*).

authoritarian religion marked the organisation of the
base for the expansion of the authority of the Roman
state. But it also extended to a much more rigorous
division of the countryside than anything produced by
the Greeks or Etruscans. As in the temple complex, the
axis rules; as with the temple precinct, the square is
the ideal. So ideally the fields were defined by a square
grid of oriented routes echoed by the streets of the
town. The main lines of external communication – the
lateral one called decumanus, the longitudinal one
cardo – continued through the town gates at the cardinal points to the quarters of authority at their intersection in the centre.

In the assertion of Rome's authority, the capitols
dominating the main forums of the colonial towns
reproduced the Temple of Jupiter Capitolinus' triad of
cellas dedicated to Jupiter, Juno and Minerva. Sometimes each had a separate building, as at Sbeitla in
Tunisia where the forum and its temples were completed towards the end of the 1st century AD.[63] By then,
of course, the style of Roman architecture had been
transformed.

63 **Sbeitla (Sufetula), forum and capitol** 1st century AD.

**64 Rome, Forum Boarium, so-called Temple of
Fortuna Virilis** early 1st century BC.
  The elegant Ionic structure of tufa and travertine
probably replaced Etruscan work on the original podium.

During her early centuries of struggle for survival and dominance in Italy, the rude town on the Tiber had acquired a veneer of Greek civilisation through the Etruscans and from direct contact with the Greek colonies of Campania. In the last quarter of the last millennium BC, after Magna Graecia had been absorbed and the Hellenistic world was being conquered, Rome herself was conquered by Hellenism – overwhelmed, indeed, by the flood of trophies taken from Hellas and the Hellenistic kingdoms of Asia.

Rome first clashed with a Hellenistic power when she turned on Macedonia to punish its king for his support of Carthage. This was effected in 197 BC and the Greek states exchanged Macedonian for Roman protection. This alarmed Antiochus III of Syria, who was beaten in 190. After renewed trouble, Macedonia was destroyed as a kingdom in 167 and annexed in 148, the Greek protectorates soon being incorporated into the province. At about the same time the Seleucids lost most of Mesopotamia to the Parthians, who had overrun Iran earlier in the century. The remaining Seleucid territory in Anatolia was under pressure from Pergamon in the west and Pontus to the north. Pergamon passed to Rome on the death of Attalus III in 133. The challenge of the Pontine king, Mithridates, who fomented rebellion in many Greek cities, was first met by the great Roman general Sulla in Greece in 85, and defeated finally by Pompey some 20 years later. Pompey dispatched the last Seleucid in 64 and made the rump of his empire into the province of Syria. Egypt followed just over 30 years later, at the end of the republic.

A clash of cultures

Though austere in her own beliefs, Rome was tolerant of other traditions provided they were not perceived to be a threat to the state. The Hellenic conception of order in design was not difficult to reconcile with native Roman ways. However, the city-state constitution could not cope with absorbing kingdoms and empires that were themselves decadent, and its society could not comprehend the material wealth and exotic attitudes of Asia and Egypt. With them came a taste for luxury and a self-indulgent sensualism inimical to the puritan ethic at the base of the Roman tradition of authority – the authority of right and duty, of the father, and of the polity, to which self-sacrifice was the supreme virtue.

The Greek stoics provided a philosophical basis for submission to the laws of Nature, which conservative Romans readily equated with Numen. However, many in the populace at large – whose ranks were swelled in Rome itself by immigrants – now sought their own salvation in the afterlife promised by eastern mystery cults such as those of Osiris/Serapis and Isis. And here on earth, credit was accorded to the victor personally rather than to Jupiter or the genius of Rome. Hellenisation lent grace to Rome's fabric, but corrupted its republic.

Corruption of the political system

Until the middle of the 2nd century BC Rome was generally reluctant to extend direct rule over defeated territories unless they were uncivilised, preferring instead to leave them to govern themselves as allies or protectorates. However, the extinction of the kingdom of Macedonia led to the development of a provincial system of fundamental significance. Apart from its effect on moral authority, annexation in the east changed the basis of power in practice. Provinces were governed by magistrates acting on behalf of the consuls (pro-consuls): unlike consuls, however, pro-consuls were not paired, their terms were often extended by popular demand and the greatest of them ruled in place of divine monarchs. Allied to the command of triumphant armies – professional standing armies rather than citizens' forces since the reforms of Marius at the end of the 2nd century BC – and fabulous booty, this was the basis for extraordinary power.

Venality was not long in corrupting the senate. With decadent government in Rome, loyalty to the state ceded to loyalty to the bountiful commander whose personal ambition was readily confused with reform. With the city-state in perpetual crisis, the usual officers of state were often superseded – most notably by Sulla, Pompey and Julius Caesar.

Caesar had helped Pompey impose his eastern settlement in 62 BC, but in a state of civil war, the two inevitably fell out when Caesar returned from the conquest of Gaul (France) with immense power and won the dictatorship in 49. Seemingly bent on holding the position for life, he was assassinated in 44 by a faction of senators who claimed commitment to the cause of republican orthodoxy against monarchy. Chaos followed. The most unlikely contender, Caesar's young nephew and adopted son Octavian (the future emperor Augustus), emerged predominant from the fray over the favourite, Mark Antony, who famously lost himself to indolence with Cleopatra in newly conquered Egypt.

The architecture of the capital

The Hellenisation of Rome was nowhere more prominently displayed than in the rebuilding of the great Temple of Jupiter Capitolinus after 83 BC to the old plan (see 57, page 118) but with the Corinthian columns pillaged by Sulla from Cossutius' Athenian Temple of Olympian Zeus (see 40, pages 88–89). Below was the Forum Romanum, the nuclear market and meeting place from which the wayward pattern of streets took its departure. As Hellenisation advanced with the complexity of urban society and the development of structural technology, the forum was surrounded by a magnificent series of buildings for the various offices of state and other specialised purposes, in addition to temples. However, it was never to be reformed along strictly regular lines.

Little survives from the earliest phases of the Forum Romanum. However, the combination of primitive form and Hellenistic order is well represented by the small Ionic temple on the Forum Boarium beside the Tiber, which survives intact.[64] Less complete is the Corinthian Temple of Vesta – the goddess personifying the numen of the hearth fire – at Tivoli,[65] which takes the elemental form of the conical hut to heights excelled only in the theatral temple at Palestrina.

Palestrina

Though Roman liturgy – like Greek – included ritual dancing, there seems to have been no drama until the 3rd century BC. Thereafter drama played a significant enough part for theatres to be incorporated in the design of sanctuaries, most spectacularly at Palestrina.[66] As in several other late republican sanctuaries, the authority of the axis is reinforced by a succession of forms revealed progressively, but here the richness of their variety is unprecedented: the columned hall at

65 **Tivoli, Temple of Vesta** first half of 1st century BC.

The form may be indigenous, but the influence of the Greek tholos in disciplining it is inescapable. The adoption of a stylobate in place of a podium is obviously a response to the circular form. The cella is an early example of concrete construction.

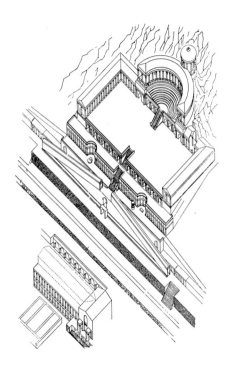

66 **Palestrina (Praeneste), Temple of Fortuna Primigenia** late 2nd or early 1st century BC, reconstructed axonometric.

Other notable late republican terraced sanctuaries are those of Hercules Victor at Tivoli (second quarter of the 1st century BC) and Jupiter Anxur at Terracina (c. 80 BC). Unlike the latter, where strength is naked, the arcades at Palestrina were concealed behind colonnades or embellished with an applied Order, as at Tivoli. The barrel vaults of the hemicycles in the intermediate terrace are among the earliest surviving examples of coffering: the progressive thinning of the membrane achieved by pouring the concrete on formwork overlaid with timber plates diminishing in size and bent to the profile of its centring. Though distorted by the curvature, the resulting grid pattern was doubtless inspired by a traditional timber structure of joists and beams.

The earliest-known precedent for the incorporation of a theatral element in the design of a sanctuary is provided by the so-called Temple of Juno at Gabii (late 3rd or early 2nd century BC). There, however, the cavea stepped back from the outer edge of the terrace, before a rectangular temple, as in the sanctuary of Hercules Victor at Tivoli.

the lowest level, the diagonal ramps, the orthogonal stairs which cut through the superimposed terraces, the barrel-vaulted hemicycles, the colonnaded precinct, the semi-circular theatral element with its enclosing colonnade, and the circular temple at the top. Recalling Pergamon (see 34, page 78), the terraces are carried on monumental arcades, and these at least remain as witness to the former magnificence.

Before Palestrina, early Hellenisation is best studied at Pompeii. The Greek grid was applied in a rudimentary way there – perhaps by natives, perhaps by Etruscans – in the last quarter of the 6th century BC and expanded with much more assurance in the 5th century.[67] As its formal arrangement demonstrates, the forum had a dual origin: it was a meeting and market place, but it was also a ceremonial space, axial in its planning, derived from the temple precinct. One of the earliest representatives of the type, the Pompeian forum stands at the head of a distinguished line of urban spaces dominated by a temple and flanked by stoa-like colonnades in front of shops and civic buildings.[68–69] Authority is here – as everywhere in the Roman conception of planning – but the Hellenisation of style was advanced at Pompeii in both public and private buildings.[70]

Apart from the temple, the palace and (later) the nymphaeum and triumphal arch, the main Roman public building types – the basilica, the council chamber and guildhall, the market building, the thermal bath house and palaestra, the theatre and amphitheatre – all appear in monumental form first in Campania, where the Hellenic and Italic traditions met. The

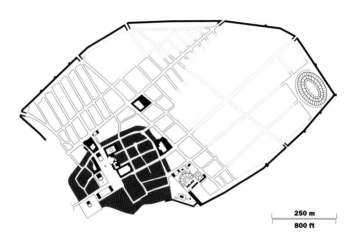

250 m
800 ft

67 **Pompeii** plan of town showing phases of development.

The central nucleus (shaded), where the forum and main
public buildings were developed, was laid out on a low hill
in the 6th century BC. The quarters to the north and east
were developed probably after the Etruscans were defeated
by the Greeks at Cumae in 474 BC, possibly after their loss
of Capua to the Samnites in 423. After Rome had
suppressed the revolt of her Italic allies in the so-called
Social War, a veterans' colony was established at Pompeii
in 80 BC and the eastern quarter was further extended
to accommodate the amphitheatre with its adjoining
gladiatorial palaestra.

Buried and substantially preserved by the eruption of
Vesuvius in AD 79, Pompeii is related to the Campanian
Greek settlements from which the Etruscans derived urban
order. Something of a grid is apparant even in the original
nucleus, but the regularity of the rectangular blocks
increased as the town grew – where existing roads allowed.
Clearly representing the synthesis of temple compound and
marketplace, the forum at the heart of the old town was
strictly reformed in the second half of the 2nd century BC.

68 **Pompeii** plan of centre.

(1) Forum; (2) capitolium; (3) Temple of Apollo;
(4) Temple of Venus; (5) basilica; (6) curia (senate house)
and magistrates' halls; (7) voting hall; (8) Eummachia's
building, dedicated to Concordia Augusta and used as the
clothiers' hall; (9) Temple of Vespasian; (10) Treasury and
Sacrarium of the Lares (shrine of the city's tutelary deities);
(11) fish or meat market; (12) theatre complex with (a) open
theatre, (b) closed odeon, (c) palaestra; (13) Temple of
Hercules with so-called Triangular Forum; (14) Temple
of Isis (Roman Fortuna); (15) Temple of Zeus Meilichios;
(16–18) Stabian, Central and Forum Baths with palaestra,
swimming pool (natatio), changing room (apodyterium),
cold room (frigidarium), warm room (tepidarium),
hot room (calidarium), women's quarters, latrine;
(19–21) houses of the Faun, Pansa and the Vettii with
entrance porch (vestibulum) or passage (prothyrum),
atrium with impluvium sometimes bordered by columns,
wing (ala), main reception room (tablinum) often open
to the garden but with side passage (fauces), dining room
(triclinium) usually with benches on three sides, bedrooms
(cubicula), peristyle, main private living/dining room
(oecus), kitchen.

The formal Hellenisation of the forum began about the

middle of the 2nd century BC. The original tufa colonnades
were in the process of reconstruction in travertine when the
city was severly damaged by earthquake in AD 62 and the
work remained incomplete when Vesuvius erupted in AD 79.
The Temple of Jupiter to the north, rebuilt in Hellenistic
form with the forum and adapted for the triad of the Roman
Temple of Jupiter Capitolinus after the establishment of
the Roman colony in 80 BC, was severely damaged in the
earthquake and was still being restored in AD 79. The
Temple of Apollo was built earlier and escaped serious
damage. The basilica and the three halls associated with the
curia, built as an adjunct to the new forum in the second half
of the 2nd century, also suffered heavily in the earthquake
and were still being restored in 79. The Temple of Isis,
the larger theatre (with uncovered seating for 5000 on
earthworks) and the Stabian Baths were probably built in
the last quarter of the 2nd century BC, though the baths were
extended after 80 BC and the theatre was modernised under
Augustus for popular spectacles (with improved access and
an integrated stage building). All were badly damaged in the
earthquake, and it is testimony to the popularity of mystery
cults that the Temple of Isis was one of the few buildings
completely renovated between AD 62 and 79. The smaller
theatre (a concert hall of concrete with seating for 1000

ruins of Pompeii include substantial remains of each
of them.

The basilica and the market building

The basilica takes primacy, and the one to the south-
west of the Pompeian forum is the earliest-known representative of a long-lived type – the first in which
internal space took precedence over external form.[71]
Greek in name but unknown in Hellas before the

under a timber roof) and the Forum Baths date from the
early years of the colony: damaged in 62, they were in use
again by 79. The buildings on the east side of the forum date
from the imperial period, the Temple of Vespasian and the
Sacrarium of the Lares, like the unfinished Central Baths
further east, from after the earthquake.

The houses of Pansa and the Faun date back to the mid
2nd century BC, the House of the Vettii to nearly a century
later. Obviously there were important changes in the course
of the relatively long lives of the earlier ones, at least: in
particular, the second atrium in the House of the Faun
seems to have been the nucleus of a separate house and its
incorporation marks the introduction of columns around
the impluvium.

69 **Pompeii** overview of model from the south-west, showing the basilica (bottom right) and forum (upper centre) (Naples, Archaeological Museum).

70 **Pompeii, Temple of Isis** view into the precinct from
the sole entrance in the north-eastern corner.

Rebuilt after the earthquake of AD 62 on the lines of a
pre-colonial shrine, the cloistered precinct appropriate to
a mystery cult contained the small, freestanding prostyle
temple of the goddess herself, the shrine of her son Horus/
Harpocrates aligned with it in the centre of the eastern
colonnade, an external altar and in the south-eastern corner
a chapel with stairs to a reservoir of water from the Nile.
Behind the western colonnade were rooms for the
ceremonies associated with initiation to the mysteries.

advent of the Romans, despite its affinity to the peristyle, the inverted peripteral form was devised for public assembly and adapted for the administration of justice. A central nave, flanked by aisles for communication, was dominated from the end opposite the door by a recessed dais elevating the seat of the presiding authority. Variations on the theme served other civic and commercial purposes.

The peristyle also produced the market building and palaestra. The Campanian addition to the former was an easily sluiced central rotunda for the dressing of meat or fish. Borrowed from the Greeks, the palaestra – as the exercise ground for sport – was an invariable adjunct to other buildings for recreation and entertainment: theatre, amphitheatre and baths.

71 **Leptis Magna, Severan Basilica** dedicated in AD 216, interior view of ruins.

Instead of the raised tribune before the flat plane of the back wall, as at Pompeii, the seat of authority in imperial basilicas usually had a dais in an apse projecting beyond the main volume, after the pattern of the Pompeian curia. Here there was an apse at each end.

The theatre and amphitheatre

The Romans promoted both sport and drama initially
as media of religious devotion – like the Greeks – and
later as popular entertainment. The forms of theatre
for both were borrowed from the Greeks, who usually
sited them on curved hillsides or earthworks. The
Roman development of the theatre type depended on
the exploitation of the arch, though earthworks
remained fundamental well into the last century BC, as
in the Circus Maximus Rome. As in Hellas, earth and
rock were supplemented first by timber and paint, then
by stone. The theatral Temple of Fortuna Primigenia at
Palestrina is the supreme example of the development
of a precipitous site with varied masonry structures on
a series of terraces (see 66, pages 138–39). At Pompeii – in
addition to the large semi-circular theatre of c. 120 BC
and in like association with a palaestra providing for
accommodation and exercise – the elliptical amphitheatre first appears as an arena for large-scale ex-
hibitions of combat between men and beasts.[72]

The baths

The Greeks bathed in cubicles with simple troughs, but
the salutary volcanic springs of Campania prompted

72 OVERLEAF **Pompeii, amphitheatre** c. 80 BC, view
with palaestra.

   Little damaged in the earthquake of AD 62, the
amphitheatre's seating for 12,000 rests on earthern
embankments – 135 by 107 metres (443 by 351 feet) –
retained by concrete arcades. Unlike its great imperial
descendants, therefore, there is no system of internal spaces
or communication. Officials entered their seats in the lowest
row through special tunnel-like corridors at ground level;
most of the public gained access up external staircases,
doubled on the western side. Rome had no comparable
facility until half a century later.

   Recalling the age-old association of sport and theatre
with religion, the Samnites had built their theatre in the
vicinity of Pompeii's oldest shrines (to Hercules and Zeus)
and incorporated two palaestrae in the complex – the larger
southern one primarily for athletics, the smaller northern
one for wrestling (later shortened for the precinct of Isis).
Enclosed by porticoes under Augustus, the vast palaestra
beside the amphitheatre augmented these facilities and
included a swimming pool.

the elaboration of the exercise in temperature-controlled complexes. Bathing for health and hygiene was combined with sport and social intercourse. Monumental formality was to supervene in imperial Rome, but in late-Samnite Campania the arrangement was essentially pragmatic: behind shops and beyond the palaestra, dressing and massage rooms adjoined a sequence of cold, warm and hot halls ranged side by side. Pompeii's baths are all like this.

The Stabian Baths are the earliest, and the complex incorporates the earliest substantially surviving domical vaults.[73] When the baths were first built, braziers in the halls themselves heated air and water as required. Soon after 80 BC, however, they were converted to the more efficient, cleaner hypocaust system, with subterranean boilers producing hot air and steam for circulation through ducts in the concrete floors and walls, as in the new Forum Baths.[74] As there, the concrete was lavishly masked – the floors with marble or mosaics, the walls with frescoes or stucco, and the vaults with painting and stucco.[75]

73 **Pompeii, Stabian Baths, frigidarium** end of 2nd century BC.

74 **Pompeii, Forum Baths, calidarium** C. 80 BC, view to
southern end with hot-water plunge bath.

75 **Pompeii, Forum Baths, tepidarium** detail of vault
with stucco decoration renovated after AD 62.
  Typically, human and animal motifs are supported by
stylised flora.

The town house

As a macrocosm, the town finds its reflection in the microcosm of the house. Like the Greek one, the Roman town house (domus) usually had a blind front to the insalubrious street or was set back behind shops.[76] Exceptionally, some of the most sumptuous houses had upper storeys with windows or even colonnades overlooking the street. The introverted form submits to the authority of the axis, and the forum as breathing and congregational space clearly has its domestic counterparts in the atrium and peristyle.

Though first discovered in Campania, the Italic atrium is generally associated with the Etruscans (see 53, page 112). The peristyle, borrowed from the Greeks for the ordering of the old walled garden, becomes increasingly important in the centuries of pervasive Hellenism. Attracting the private rooms, including a summer dining room (oecus, also of Greek derivation), it was to eclipse the atrium as pressure of population growth reduced the space available to house-builders. By the end of the republic, the two were ideally aligned on axis through the tablinum, as in the Pompeian houses of Pansa or the Menander.[77]

76 **Herculaneum** overview of the ruins showing atrium
houses (centre) and the street elevations of houses in the
background.

Herculaneum suffered the same fate as Pompeii in AD 79.

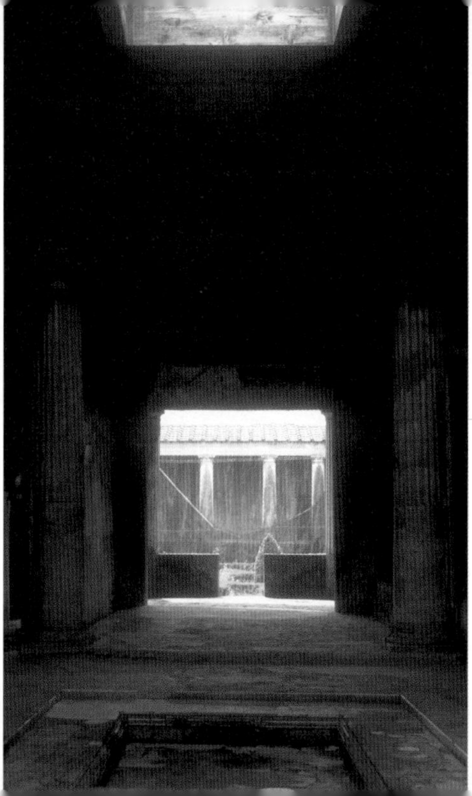

Property extension led to variation, as in the houses of the Faun and the Vettii, and from the 1st century BC extension was often effected illusionistically in paint (see 80, pages 168–69). Most walls were painted, sometimes above marble dados, and most floors were paved in marble or mosaic.

The villa

Axial planning was so pervasive with the Romans that they even took it with them to the country, despite their appreciation of nature and the relatively relaxed context of life there. Two main types of country house (villa) developed: the estate house with considerable accommodation, and the relaxed retreat, often near town or by the sea. Primarily for recreation or entertainment rather than extended residence, the latter were the most sumptuous in their

77 Pompeii, House of the Menander view through the atrium to the peristyle.

Absent from Etruscan house tombs, the trough sunk into the floor below the compluvium – the norm in later Campania – seems to have come from the Hellenistic east with the peristyle.

internal spatial variety, while at the same time remaining sensitive to the natural qualities of their surroundings.

The seaside villa usually had a range of facilities – living rooms, reception rooms, baths, terraces, et cetera – informally devolved along the shore. In countryside and suburb it was common to build on platforms to raise the rooms to enjoy the view. By the end of the 1st century BC the most lavish villas had several terraced platforms, aligned or freely disposed in accordance with the contours of the site. The so-called Villa of the Mysteries outside Pompeii[78] is an outstanding example of the platform type. On an arcaded podium, it had a symmetrical plan around a court and seems to have been surrounded by porticos on three sides from the outset. A peristyle was added later on the north-easterly fourth side and later still, possibly following the introduction of glazing in the 1st century AD, a semi-circular extension was projected into the garden on the main axis, beyond the south-west portico. The villa takes its name from the fresco cycle, supposedly representing Dionysiac rites, which decorates one of the rooms.

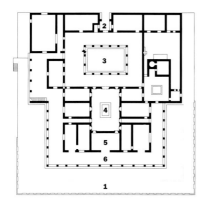

78 Pompeii, Villa of the Mysteries before 150 BC.
(1) Arcaded podium with cryptoporticos; (2) central entrance; (3) internal garden court with peristyle added later; (4) atrium; (5) tablinum; (6) external portico with view.

The villa seems to have been extended and redecorated in the late 2nd or early 1st century BC and again in the middle of the 1st century AD. When the peristyle was added the original court became an atrium, in reverse of the usual entrance sequence (as Vitruvius, VI.5, requires in villas).

Decoration

Various permutations of style have been distinguished in the painted decoration of the houses at Pompeii and elsewhere in the Hellenised Roman republic. The first style, current c. 200 to 80 BC and reflecting Hellenistic fashion, imitated polychrome marble revetment in dividing wall surfaces into a dado and panels with moulded frames, a frieze and/or cornice. It was tectonic if not yet architectonic, though pilaster panels were occasionally included. Then, for two or three generations after Pompeii became a colony in 80 BC, the fully architectonic second style denied the wall and feigned increasingly complex extensions of space scenographically,[79-80] as in the theatre. Ultimately these framed illusory views of garden or countryside, often as the setting for figures in mythological episodes. The figures were sometimes brought forward and enlarged, eclipsing their context like players on a stage, as in the Villa of the Mysteries.[81] Thereafter theatricality reigned.

The tenement block

With the growth of both the town and the economy in the 1st century AD, the pattern of housing had to

79 **Rome, Palatine, second-style decoration in the House of Augustus**.

80 OVERLEAF **Pompeii, second-style decoration**
architectural illusionism of the type developed for the skene in the Greek theatre and copied by the Romans (Naples, National Museum).

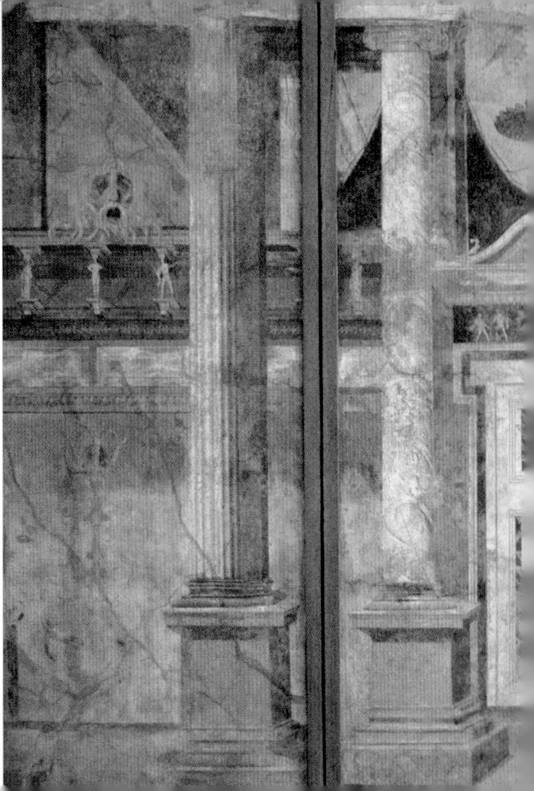

change. The rich resorted to their villas. For those of the expanding middle class who could afford a town house (domus), the type with a grand atrium as well as a peristyle was old-fashioned by the time Pompeii was destroyed. Now the atrium was reduced to little more than a vestibule and the peristyle predominated, often with more than one storey of accommodation around it. Given crowded conditions and advanced building technology, the less affluent majority lived in multi-storey tenements (insulae).[82]

Recorded as early as the late 3rd century BC, though still regarded as a Roman phenomenon by Vitruvius, blocks of flats were also to be developed on a grand scale in Ostia and elsewhere in the imperial period. Built around courtyards of varied dimensions, they usually had single-level apartments superimposed on three or more storeys over shops and lit by windows

81 **Pompeii, Villa of the Mysteries, early second-style decoration** part of scene IX (a flagellation ritual beginning on the neighbouring wall), c. 60 BC.

After a Greek original, the figures were painted on to a late first-style decorative scheme possibly inherited from an earlier phase of the building.

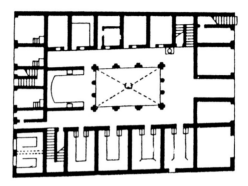

82 **Typical Roman tenement block (insula)** plan and
reconstruction.

Anticipated by the multi-storey house, the insula became
the major urban building type with the improvement of
brick and concrete building technology. Between three and
five storeys were common. Raised from the street by shops
but relatively easily accessible and usually taller than the
levels above, the first floor was considered the best location.
The courtyards varied in extent in accordance with the

general affluence of the proprietors, but in all types were
usually surrounded by arcaded galleries of communication
with staircases in the corners. Left unsheathed in an
essentially extroverted and utilitarian genre, the brick
exteriors depended on the relationship between window
and plane wall. Glass was introduced to the more luxurious
blocks before the middle of the 2nd century BC. Flexible,
the form was adaptable to many purposes from offices to
warehouses – like its multi-storey metal and glass successor
in the 20th century.

overlooking the street. Many were prey to squatters, who erected shanties on their roofs in inflammable materials. Augustan reform limited the height of buildings in Rome to 21 metres (70 feet) and imposed fire regulations, but their impact on the existing fabric was obviously limited and much of the city was destroyed in the famous fire of AD 64. Far from having been in any way personally responsible, the Emperor Nero attempted to regulate rebuilding, widening and straightening streets, lining them with colonnades, enforcing the earlier height restriction, increasing the distance between buildings, ensuring their structural integrity and limiting the use of inflammable materials (Tacitus, *Annals*, XV, 43). But the problems of enforcement must have been insuperable.

The advance of building technology under the Romans, like their planning, related directly to the discipline of their military life and the authority of their administration: to move vast armies required great organisational skill, not only in regimenting people but in developing transportation and service facilities. The authority of the Roman road and aqueduct was established in 312 BC, when the magistrate Appius Claudius built the Aqua and Via Appia. Largely at ground level, the former was the first of 14 great channels for the city's water supply. The latter connected Rome to Capua and the conquered cities of Campania. Pressed on, the way was paved to the towns of Magna Graecia and the ports of embarkation for conquest overseas. As the legions advanced so too did the roads, deviating as little as possible from the authoritarian line – even in the undulating islands of Britain.

Of course, roads and aqueducts had to cross chasms of various sizes, and this produced awe-inspiring arches. Discipline is again implied in the submission to the authority of structure, to the authority of engineering as a means for the expansion of the authority of the state. Nowhere is this better illustrated than by the great structure built c. 19 BC to

carry a road as well as a water channel over the river Gard to Nimes in the south of France.[83] Nowhere is there a more splendid testimony to the perseverance of Roman ashlar masonry – and to the beauty of functional design.

Other utilitarian arcuate structures included market halls and warehouses for the storage of foodstuffs, and sewers. As much of Rome's grain had to be imported from at least as early as the 5th century BC, granaries must have been built from this time. How-

83 PREVIOUS PAGES **Nimes, Pont du Gard** c. 19 BC.
Built entirely of stone, the triple-storey bridge – carrying a road at first level and the slab-covered water channel at the top – is 269 metres (882 feet) long and 49 metres (61 feet) high. Its superimposed arcades represent the apotheosis of a tradition of utilitarian public works dating back to the Pons Aemilius (142 BC), the overground Aqua Marcia (144 BC) and beyond. Often using pipes, occasionally pumps, the essentially practical Romans kept their aqueducts just above or below ground level wherever possible. This one great structure over the Gard enabled them to do this for virtually all the rest of the 50 kilometres (31 miles) between the springs of Uzès and Nimes.

ever, the earliest large-scale Roman warehouse is
thought to be the Porticus Aemilia – 49 by 87 metres
(160 by 285 feet) – by the Tiber below the Aventine,
which may have been built as early as 174 or even 193
BC. Rome had sewers in Etruscan times: dating from
the 6th century BC, the main one (Cloaca Maxima) was
vaulted at the end of the 2nd century. Flat slabs long
remained the norm for covering drains.

Materials and structure

The Romans of the republican era rarely used costly
building materials – even for temples. They learned
from the Etruscans to build their major public works
from finely dressed blocks of stone whose dead weight
held them together. By the 3rd century BC they had
developed a hard-setting mortar made of volcanic
sand (*pozzolana*), lime and water, which freed them
from reliance on the dead weight of massive blocks.
Well before the middle of the 2nd century they were
mixing this mortar with light rubble to make a primitive concrete, and forming walls by laying it between
courses of brick or stones which could be set in increasingly intricate and regular patterns because all the
strength lay in the bond.[84] By c. 100 temple walls were

occasionally of tufa, but generally of concrete sheathed in tufa or travertine and plastered and painted. Orders were usually of travertine – the imported marble columns of the Roman Temple of Jupiter Capitolinus were, of course, exceptional.

The lightness and malleability of concrete not only made construction easier and cheaper, but poured over a temporary timber mould (centring) for arch and vault,[85] it prompted a radical advance in the conception of form. The principle of the arch was simply extended to form the semi-circular barrel or tunnel vault and then turned on its centre to form the semi-spherical domical vault.[86] The Stabian Baths in Pompeii (see 73, page 157) had both types of vault before the end of the 2nd century BC. New standards of concrete construction and spatial diversity were set by the Pompeian Forum Baths soon after 80 BC (see 74, page 158) and later developments depended on moulded concrete to distinguish the various stages of the bathing process.

The development of the architecture of space, which took its departure from buildings such as the Stabian Baths, is a distinct issue of fundamental importance to the whole tradition of architecture, and we shall deal

84 **Revetment of opus caementum (mortared rubble).**

FROM LEFT TO RIGHT *Opus incertum* (irregular patchwork); *opus reticulatum* (chequerboard); *opus testaceum* (brick).

The main trend in masonry was towards greater regularity, though polygonal work subsisted with squared ashlar due to abundant cheap limestone quarried north of Rome which split irregularly. Tufa and travertine quarried in Latium cut readily into rectangular blocks and were used either in solid blocks or more often in sheets as revetment for the concrete walls of temples and other prestigious buildings.

85 **Construction of an arched bridge on timber centring.**

with it as such. On the other hand, following the Hellenistic lead with no less significance for the future, the Romans also realised the full implications of the column's abstraction from its structural role and its application to the wall as an articulating agent. To conclude this account of Hellenistic architecture, its inheritance and legacy, we shall trace the lengths to which they went.

86 **Vaulting.**

FROM LEFT TO RIGHT Barrel; groin; domical.

The advent of the new architecture of space towards the end of the 1st millennium BC coincided with the reformation of the empire by Julius Caesar's heir, Octavian. Having defeated Antony and Cleopatra and the decadent east in 31 BC, he surrendered to a purged senate. Accorded the title of Augustus[87] and elevated to lead the college of priests (as pontifex maximus), he promoted a return to old values and could ultimately claim to have restored the republic. From 27 BC until his death in AD 14 he was re-endowed annually with the disposal of the consulship (which gave him prime authority) and with the tribunian power (which gave him popular appeal). His most effective endowment, however, was a general proconsular imperium which ran to supreme command of the armed forces. Called princeps (first citizen), in principle he left the senate to decide whether his extraordinary accumulation of powers would survive him. In fact, however, he set the precedent for nominating his heir from within his family, and his adopted family name – Caesar – came to be associated with the position for ever after.

87 **Augustus** marble statue from Prima Porta (Rome, Vatican Museums).

Augustus reformed the army, stationing divisions in permanent camps around the frontiers, and developed a professional civil service, drawn mainly from the middle class. But the effectiveness of the Augustan system depended in part on the character of the princeps, and without a generally accepted formula for disposing of the position, the succession was insecure – to the cost of both dynasty and empire. Adoption was obviously calculated to save the succession from falling hostage to the fortune (or ill-fortune) of birth, but it certainly did not prevent inter-family rivalry from favouring the inadequate. Augustus adopted his successor, the much-maligned Tiberius (AD 14–37), but rivalry within his Julio-Claudian dynasty had reputedly eliminated many good men before the succession of the infamous Caligula (37–41) and the spoilt Nero (54–68). In between, the army set an ominous precedent in promoting Claudius – though he proved to be well advised and a competent ruler. After the assassination of Nero, military might triumphed with the authoritarian Vespasian (69–79), who had no time for the fiction of a restored republic.

Having instituted a hereditary monarchy, Vespasian

was succeeded by his sons Titus and Domitian. But the latter's autocratic style provoked his murder (in AD 96), and the ultimate legatee was another great soldier, Trajan (AD 98–117), who was no less a monarch. After Trajan, adoption, birth and the army – even the senate – all produced emperors, and for more than a century most of them were creditable. Indeed, it would be hard to account for the empire's survival if the general level of probity were fairly represented by the lurid records of anti-imperial propagandists (like Suetonius), appeasement of the popular taste for cruel barbarity notwithstanding.

The genius of Rome

Restoring confidence in Rome, Augustus established the basis for a revival of the old religion and its mores. A key element in his policy was state sponsorship of Virgil and the revival of epic literature which acknowledged the common origins of the Roman and the Greek but asserted the triumph of the Latin genius in glorifying the destiny of Rome. Tolerance of other beliefs was sustained, but foreign cults were rigorously excluded from the sacred boundaries of the metropolis. Yet the traditional devotion to the genius of Rome

acquired an eastern aspect in its identification with Caesar – the so-called cult of the emperor.

The genius of Rome was embodied in a long line of venerable men, personifications of her mores. As heirs to Virgil's hero Aeneas they might be seen as super-human in the light of Greek mythology, but the idea of man becoming god – of his apotheosis – was one of the exotic eastern imports which appalled puritanical republicans. In the place of the Hellenistic king, however, Romans did achieve apotheosis: in the east, recently renewed tradition attributed divinity – at least of inspiration – to the ruler who sustained his mandate in furthering prosperity and security. In the newly set-tled west, on the other hand, civilisation, prosperity and security were due to Rome. Thus meaning differ-ent things in different places, the cult of Rome and Augustus was generally maintained as the affirmation of dedication to the imperial ideal.

Temples were dedicated to Rome and Augustus after his death, and many of his successors were simi-larly honoured – as was his uncle, Julius Caesar. But

88 Rome, Forum Romanum general view through the Arch of Titus to the Arch of Septimius Severus.

the building type specifically designed to celebrate the apotheosis of imperial power was the triumphal arch.[88] Extracted from the city gate to mark the sacred way of triumph to the Temple of Jupiter Capitolinus in cities all over the empire, as in Rome, the triumphal arch was the Hellenised form of the old Mesopotamian twin-towered palace portal, where divinity appeared before man through the agency of the king. The Roman commemorative arch goes back at least to the triumph of Scipio Africanus in the Carthaginian wars (146 BC), but the classical form appears with Augustus, if not Julius Caesar.

A city of marble

The moral regeneration of the Augustan age was supported by a regeneration of the arts – not least architecture. Inspired by the grand plans of his uncle and

89 Rome, Forum of Julius Caesar (Forum Julium) with Temple of Venus Genetrix dedicated 46 BC but completed under Augustus, imaginative reconstruction.

   With its entrance portico and twin colonnades, Caesar's forum completes the process of Hellenisation advanced in the forum at Pompeii. Planned after its patron's victory

over Pompey in 48 BC and dedicated two years later to
the goddess from whom the Julian line traced its descent,
the temple was flanked by the pair of triumphal arches
which doubtless commemorate victory over external and
internal enemies.

90 **Imperial Rome, Forum Romanum and imperial forums** (model in the Museum of Roman Civilisation, Rome).

aided by his great minister, Agrippa, Augustus was vig-
orous in his determination to renovate the fabric as
well as the polity of Rome – and the spoils of conquest
provided a seemingly inexhaustible fund. Utilitarian
public works were not neglected but in his testament,
Res Gestae, Augustus claimed to have found the capital a city of brick and left it a city of marble. The trans-
formation was effected by opening the quarries at
Carrara. The new material called for neo-Hellenic
standards of detail and craftsmanship – indeed the importation of craftsmen from Greece – which gave the
era a classicising image despite the wide diversity of its
buildings. And the emperor endowed Athens in return.

Agrippa's major effort was concentrated on developing the area around the Campus Martius, to the
west of the Capitoline, with forums, porticos, baths, a
basilica and the Pantheon. Augustus was responsible
for many buildings, but his major thrust was focused
on the programme of renovation and extension initiated by his uncle around the Forum Romanum. Emulating Julius Caesar, whose temple and forum mark the
complete regularisation of the old Italic tradition,[89] he
began the ultimately extensive sequence of imperial
forums to the east of the Forum Romanum[90–91] by

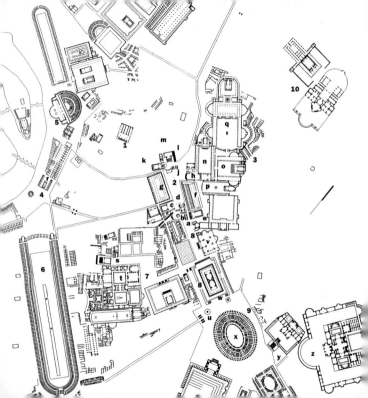

91 **Imperial Rome** plan of central area.

(1) Capitoline with the Temple of Jupiter Capitolinus (the Temple of Jupiter Optimus Maximus, Juno and Minerva, the cult centre of the city's patron deities) and site of the ancient citadel (Arx) to the north-east; (2) Forum Romanum with (a) Regia (the Etruscan royal megaron), (b) Temple of Vesta (with sacred hearth, symbol of the city's life) and neighbouring House of the Vestal Virgins, (c) Temple of Castor and Pollux, (d) Temple of Divus Julius with Arch of Augustus beside it, (e) Temple of Antoninus and Faustina, (f) Basilica Aemilia, (g) Basilica Julia, (h) curia (senate house) by place of public assembly (comitium), (i) Rostrum (for address to public assembly), (j) Arch of Septimius Severus, (k) Temple of Saturn, (l) temples of Concord and Vespasian, (m) Tabularium (state archives); (3) imperial forums: (n) Julium and Temple of Venus Genetrix, (o) Augustum and Temple of Mars Ultor, (p) Transitorium and Temple of Minerva, (q) Trajan with, from north-west to south-east, Temple of Divus Traianus and its precinct, column, Basilica Ulpia, and outer court and equestrian statue flanked by semi-circular market buildings; (4) Forum Boarium with (r) Temple of Fortuna Virilis; (5) Theatre of Marcellus by the Tiber bridge; (6) Circus Maximus; (7) Palatine with (s) House of Livia (Augustus' wife) and

other early Julio-Claudian palaces, (t) Flavian Palace, state
apartments with basilica, aula regia and lararium to the
north-east of the central peristyles, triclinium to the south-
west and private apartments and garden on lower level to
the south-east; (8) Via Sacra with (u) Arch of Constantine,
(v) Basilica of Constantine, (w) Temple of Venus and Rome,
founded by Hadrian, and Arch of Titus; (9) site of Nero's
Golden House, redeveloped for (x) Colosseum, (y) Baths
of Titus and (z) Baths of Trajan; (10) Baths of Constantine
and Serapaeum.

The Forum Romanum (2) was originally an unpaved
marketplace flanked by shops (tabernae), narrowing
towards the Via Sacra to the south-east and rising with the
slope of the Capitoline to the north-west. Public assemblies
were held in front of the curia (h). By the end of the republic
the only significant Etruscan survival (apart from the
foundations of temples) was the Regia (a) below the
Palatine. Hellenisation transformed the other public
buildings, lending order to their environment, but the
organic growth pattern was never entirely erased. The old
tabernae (cubicles with living rooms above) to the north
were destroyed by fire in 210 BC and by 179 they had been
replaced by the Basilica Aemilia behind a shopping stoa (f).
This complex was rebuilt after 55 BC by Julius Caesar, who

also rebuilt the neighbouring curia c. 45. Both were rebuilt again by Augustus after a fire in 14 BC. Beside the Temple of Castor and Pollux (c) – founded in the early 5th century BC, rebuilt in 117 and again from 7 BC – the shops along the southern side (out of alignment with those on the north) were replaced by a stoa in 169 and this in turn gave way to the Basilica Julia (g), which was built by Caesar after 54 and rebuilt with concrete vaults (rather than the usual timber ceiling) by Augustus after a fire c. 12 BC. Regularisation at the western end was inhibited by the slopes of the Capitoline hill with the Temple of Saturn (reputedly from the early 5th century BC but rebuilt c. 30 BC) to the south (k) and the public assembly ground at the base of the northern spur supporting the Arx. The asymmetrical composition was effectively closed in 78 BC by Sulla's construction of the Tabularium (m) and Caesar's relocation of the Rostrum (i) in conjunction with his work on the curia. The eastern end was closed in 29 BC by the Temple of the Divus Julius (d), which masked the irregular Etruscan distribution of the Regia (a) – restored in 36 BC – and Temple of Vesta (b). The Arch of Augustus – attached c. 19 BC to the south side of the Temple of Divus Julius to commemorate victory over the Parthians – eclipsed the Fornix Fabianus (built in 121 to commemorate victory over barbarians and rebuilt in 57), which provided the precedent for it – and, presumably, for the arches of the Forum of Julius Caesar.

   Slightly expanding the formula promoted by his uncle (see 89, page 191), but bringing the temple further forward between concave exedrae, Augustus' forum (o) marks the apogee of the regime's classicising tendency at the end of the last century BC. Craftsmen were imported from Athens to effect a neo-Hellenic precision in the handling of marble here and in the contemporary Ara Pacis (altar of peace) of the Campus Martius (Field of Mars). The surviving fragments of the forum and the virtually complete altar indicate that, along with a somewhat pedantic Hellenic historicism reproduced in new opulence, they brought with them a vital Hellenistic taste for the uncanonical in proportions and decoration. The caryatids of the surrounding colonnades represent the historicism; 'Pegasus' capitals represent uncanonical vitality. Deriving respectively from the Erechtheum on the Athenian Acropolis (see volume 2, HELLENIC CLASSICISM, page 141) and buildings like the Temple of Apollo at Didyma (see 13, page 37), both recall the inner propylaea donated to the sanctuary of Demeter at Eleusis by the Roman Appius Claudius Pulcher c. 50 BC.

   The later imperial forums are overshadowed by the great complex laid out for the Emperor Trajan by Apollodorus

of Damascus and dedicated in AD 113 (q). Developing the
formula bequeathed by Augustus, the architect provided a
rich sequence of spaces. The temple precinct to the north-
west was preceded by a colonnaded court flanked by semi-
circular market buildings with over 150 shops in addition
to a great hall of six groin-vaulted bays – 28 by 9.8 metres
(91 feet 10 inches by 32 feet 2 inches) – further up the
terraced slopes of the Quirinal hill. Between this and the
precinct was a transverse basilica (the Basilica Ulpia with
its double aisles and two apses). The outer court was
centred on an equestrian statue of the emperor and the inner
precinct was preceded by a monumental column, 38 metres
(124 feet 8 inches) high, supporting another statue of the
emperor and embellished with a spiral relief of his conquest
of Dacia.

On the Palatine (7) – the traditional residence of the
pontifex maximus, who had inherited the religious functions
of the Tarquin kings – Augustus and his wife Livia were
accommodated in relative, and much flaunted, modesty (s).
His immediate successors augmented this, but it was not
until the reign of Domitian (AD 81–96) that a truly imperial
palace (t) eclipsed all earlier work – even the seats of
Hellenistic monarchs, from which its builders drew their
inspiration though developing their own conception of space.

92 **Rome, Portico of Gaius and Lucius** late 1st century
BC, drawing of remains by Giuliano da Sangallo, late
15th century AD.

This Doric portico has been identified with the one
sheltering the shops in front of the Basilica Aemilia. If the
identification is correct, the trabeated system imposed on
the walls would have contrasted with the arcades of the
Basilica Julia on the other side of the street.

importing Athenians to create the Forum Augustum and Temple of Mars Ultor. Though a considerable amount survived to inspire the Renaissance,[92] little of all this remains now. Indeed, the most complete representatives of a varied age are the Arch of Augustus at Rimini[93] and the Maison Carrée at Nimes.[94]

Vitruvius

The theoretical basis for Augustan architecture was provided by Vitruvius Pollio, the only ancient architectural theorist whose text has descended to us intact. A military engineer in the service of Julius Caesar, he was widely travelled and knew the great sites of Greece and Asia Minor. He was also widely read and quotes numerous Greek writers among his sources. He wrote his treatise in the decade or so after Caesar's assassination, when political chaos stifled practice, and dedicated it c. 27 BC to the new princeps who promised great opportunities to architects.

The first seven of Vitruvius' ten books deal with architecture, building and decoration and the last three with mechanics and engineering. After differentiating public building from private, religious from secular and describing the ideal town, Book 1 defines

93 **Rimini, Arch of Augustus** 27 BC.

This ceremonial gate in the city wall was built to mark
the end of the restored Via Flaminia (with its twin on the
northern outskirts of Rome). The unresolved relationship
between the arch, the Order, the pediment and the putative
attic (which was to develop into a standard element of
the triumphal arch) marks the work as preceding the
promotion of Hellenic logic and precision in the mature
Augustan age.

The deletion of the pediment in the revision of the
formula for the Arch of Augustus at Susa (c. 9 BC)
effectively solved the major problem, though the
relationship between the applied Order and the arch
required further thought: with only one column set well
beyond a flat section of wall to each side of the arch, the
entablature was over-extended and the two elements merely
co-exist. The standard solution was to support the arch with
distinct piers and double the columns to frame them – as,
probably, in the Forum of Julius Caesar (see 89, page 191)
and the later Arch of Titus (see 88, page 188).

94 Nimes, the so-called Maison Carrée 1st decade AD.
This temple, the finest surviving work of the period, was
officially dedicated to Cais and Lucius Caesar as the heirs
to the princeps. The pseudo-peripteral form conforms to
the Italic norm, but the precision of the workmanship and
the details of the Order follow the example of the Temple
of Mars Ultor and the acanthus-scroll frieze that of the
Ara Pacis.

the basic principles and concerns of architecure: order, propriety and economy; strength, utility and beauty. Having traced the origins of architecture to the cave and the hut woven like a nest or won from the living tree, Book II surveys sophisticated building materials and methods. Opening the account of building types with temples, Book III defines order.

Order in composition begins with symmetry, which for Vitruvius is correspondence between the parts and the whole, drawn not merely from consistent distribution but from the consistent proportioning of dimensions in accordance with a common module (a basic unit selected as standard). The supreme exemplar is the ideal man proportioned on a grid and described by a square and circle – the key to the Hellenic identification of microcosm and macrocosm, man and universe.[95] By implication, rational geometry is the essence of complete coherence in planning – as in the ideal town.

Pursuing the analogy between architectural order and the human body, Vitruvius introduces the Orders and asserts that there are two: male and female. These are Doric and Ionic respectively, the Corinthian being an elaboration of the Ionic, the Tuscan a primitive

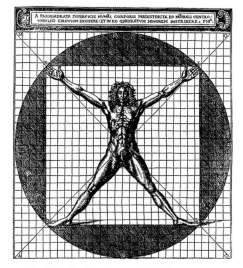

A PARIQVADRATA SVPERFICIE HVMAI CORPORIS PERDISTINCTA EO NATVRALI CENTRO VMBILICI CIRCVLVM EXCIPERE: ET IN EO QVADRATVM MINOREM INSCRIBERE. FIG.

95 **The Vitruvian ideal man and ideal town.**

   Writing 'On symmetry in temples and the human body', Vitruvius defines the essence of order as proportion: 'a correspondence among the measures of an entire work, and of the whole to a certain part selected as standard... Without symmetry and proportion there can be no

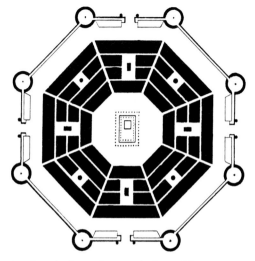

principles in the design of any temple; that is, if there is
no precise relation between its members, as in the case of
those of a well-shaped man.' After defining the ideal ratios
between the parts of the human body ('the length of the foot
is one-sixth of the height…' et cetera), he notes that 'if a
man is placed flat on his back, with his hands and feet

extended, and a pair of compasses centred at his navel, the
fingers and toes of his two hands and feet will touch the
circumference of a circle described therefrom. And just as
the human body yields a circular outline, so too a square
figure may be found from it… Therefore, since nature has
designed the human body so that its members are duly
proportioned to the frame as a whole, it appears that the
ancients had good reason for their rule that in perfect
buildings the different members must be in exact
symmetrical relations to the whole general scheme.'
(Book III.1).

As a corollary, in accounting for the origin of the Orders,
Vitruvius relates that the Dorians, 'wishing to set up
columns [for a temple to Apollo]…and being in search of
some way by which they could render them fit to bear a
load and also of a satisfactory beauty of appearance…
measured the imprint of a man's foot and compared this
with his height. On finding that, in a man, the foot was one-
sixth of the height, they applied the same principle to the
column and reared it, shaft and capital, to a height six times
its thickness at its base. Thus the Doric column, as used in
buildings, began to exhibit the proportions, strength and
beauty of the body of a man… When they desired to
construct a temple to Diana in a new style of beauty, they

translated these footprints into terms characteristic of the
slenderness of a woman…' (Book IV.1). The Doric Order
attained the proportions of 1:6 long after its maturity,
but that does not invalidate the anthropomorphic thesis.

Vitruvius' original illustrations were not reproduced
in the copies of his work which survived the collapse of
classical antiquity. New ones, many controversial, were
provided in the new editions which appeared following the
Renaissance of humanist studies and classical architecture
in 15th-century Italy. Forcing conformity between idea and
image, Cesare Cesariano's strident figure of the Vitruvian
man (Como, 1521) has some advantage over more
celebrated versions in the clarity – if unsubtlety – with
which the grid determines the proportions of the symmetry
described by square and circle.

For his ideal town, Vitruvius specifically recommends a
circular perimeter to avoid salient angles that might shelter
enemies. The towers punctuating the perimeter wall may
be circular or polygonal. Most of his editors produce a
polygonal plan for the whole. The positioning of gates
off-axis with the streets radiating from the central forum
follows from Vitruvius' determination to shut out the winds.
The approach accords with the time-honoured defensive
device of turning entrance through right angles.

translation of the Doric which merits comparatively little attention. Propriety governs their application in accordance with the virility of the dedicatee, the status of the patron and, in multi-storey civil works, the need for apparent strength at the base and lightness and grace above. Beyond that, tracing the details of both systems to timber construction, Vitruvius promotes an architectonic approach to decoration. For all his rationalism, however, he reveals an engineer's pragmatism in urging common-sense respect for the circumstances of site and programme.

The application of the Orders

It was in the context of the multi-storey buildings of their engineers – in particular the theatres or amphitheatres and stadia carried on superimposed arcades – that the Romans perfected their architectonic approach to ornament through the application of the Order to the wall as a metaphor for load and support: their synthesis of the native and Hellenistic traditions.

96 **Arles, amphitheatre** late 1st century AD, view along a typical ambulatory arcade with steps to the upper level on the right.

Mastery of the arch had achieved superimposed galleries of stone to provide support for, and access to, the cavea on flat sites.[96] The strictly semi-circular structure was closed beyond a relatively deep stage by a scenae frons in the form of a permanent palace façade integrated with and rising to the height of the cavea. The first such theatre was begun in Rome in 55 BC by Pompey. Its descendants have proved the most durable of Roman legacies.

Articulation with superimposed Orders stamped a coherent framework of proportions on the whole while differentiating each level in accordance with the prescriptions of Vitruvius – the male canon for strength and virility at the base, the female for lightness and grace above. This was most prominently displayed from c. 78 BC in the two storeys of the Tabularium which overlooked the Forum Romanum from the west. The Theatre of Marcellus, completed c. 10 BC,[97] is the earliest work surviving in substantial part in which Doric and Ionic Orders are superimposed on tiered arcades – and there was probably a Corinthian one applied to the tall parapet at the top, too. The Colosseum[98–99] is the supreme example: three tiers of arcades are framed by Doric, Ionic and Corinthian Or-

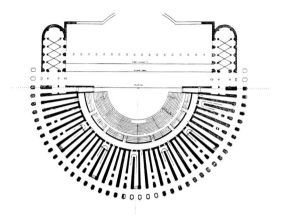

97 **Rome, Theatre of Marcellus** completed c. 10 BC,
plan, and model and detail of Order (OVERLEAF).

It is known that there were elaborate temporary theatres
in Rome in the first half of the 1st century BC – the fantasy
theatres which feature prominently in the third style of
Pompeian wall painting presumably reflect them – but there
were no permanent buildings for public entertainment there
until Pompey built his stone theatre in 55 BC. Preceded by

the large theatre of Pompeii – among many others in Magna
Graecia – it was modelled on the Hellenistic theatre at
Mitylene, but with the semi-circle closed by the diagonal
scenae frons. As at Palestrina (see 66, page 138), a peristyle ran
round the cavea at the top with a circular tempietto
in the centre, recalling the sacred origin of drama and
mollifying puritan objection to the erection of monumental
theatres. With timber seating terraced over superimposed
ambulatory arcades and divided into sectors by radiating

staircases – as at Arles – the type had clearly established itself in stone by the time of Augustus.

Conforming to precedent, the theatre named after Augustus' protégé Marcellus was planned under Caesar but not completed until towards the end of the second-last decade BC. Incorporated into a medieval fort and then into a Renaissance palace, the cavea is well preserved in part, but the scenae frons has disappeared. It is not known whether there was a third level of arcades with a Corinthian Order or a blind wall, but there were three tiers of seats accommodating about 11,000 people – the lower two of stone, the top one of timber. The seating was carried by arches ascending in height on the radii. Ramps were inserted between radiating walls at regular intervals and the external galleries, arcaded within the Orders around the circumference and radially vaulted, provided both buttressing and access to them.

A derivative of the Roman theatre type, crossed with the Greek type of the bouleterion, is the odeon: a roofed auditorium for concerts and lectures. Apart from the one at Pompeii, dating from the early years of the colony, the most prominent example is the one built by Agrippa c. 15 BC on the south-west of the Acropolis at Athens (see volume 2, HELLENIC CLASSICISM, page 116).

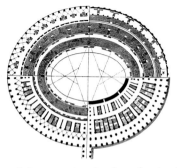

98 **Rome, Colosseum** AD 71–80, plan and sectional view.

Built on the site of Nero's notorious palace to
accommodate some 50,000 spectators, the Colosseum is
188 by 156 metres (280 by 175 feet). Unprecedented in
scale if not in form, travertine outside, tufa inside and with
concrete limited to the foundations and the upper walls
and tunnel-vaults, the awesome structure was hardly novel
towards the end of the 1st century AD. The cavea of the
Theatre of Marcellus anticipated it in most of its essentials
and the elliptical form had long been established at Pompeii
though the latest precedents in Rome were temporary
structures of Caligula and Nero.

The tiered arcades with their applied Orders doubled as

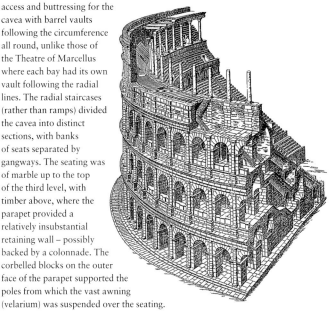

access and buttressing for the cavea with barrel vaults following the circumference all round, unlike those of the Theatre of Marcellus where each bay had its own vault following the radial lines. The radial staircases (rather than ramps) divided the cavea into distinct sections, with banks of seats separated by gangways. The seating was of marble up to the top of the third level, with timber above, where the parapet provided a relatively insubstantial retaining wall – possibly backed by a colonnade. The corbelled blocks on the outer face of the parapet supported the poles from which the vast awning (velarium) was suspended over the seating.

99 Rome, Colosseum view from the south-east.

ders of half-columns, and the parapet, blind except for
windows in every second bay, has Corinthian pilasters.

If the Roman theatre had achieved its definitive
form by the end of the 1st millennium BC, the process
of elaborating the scenae frons was endless, providing
the ideal context for an appeal to emotion through the
manipulation of form. Freed from the logic of structure, the Orders were applied to the development of a
fantastic scenography in variations on the theme of
the palace façade which anticipated the overtly theatrical baroque of 17th-century Rome. The style
recurs in many public buildings, notably the reservoir
fountains (nymphaea) which, as the source of water
for most, played a major part in the scenography of
the colonnaded street – especially in the more sophisticated east. And scenographic planning, arranging
rich vistas through various spaces as often imitated on
the stage, was characteristic of the Romans too.[100]

100 **Baalbek, sacred precinct with Temple of Jupiter
(top) and Temple of Bacchus.**

Long a cult centre of Ba'al and his offspring Tammuz (the
local vegetation/regeneration deity), who were associated
respectively with Zeus and Dionysius by Hellenistic

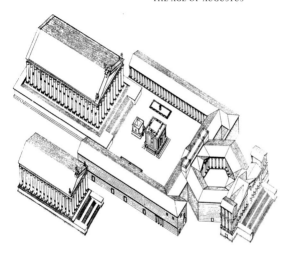

theologians, the site was preferred by the Roman governors
of Syria as a focal point of imperial devotion to Jupiter
and Bacchus – themselves the Roman equivalents to Zeus
and Dionysius. The enormous main temple to the great
Capitoline god – 48 by 88 metres (157 by 289 feet) with ten

by 19 unfluted columns rising to nearly 20 metres (66 feet) –
was built on an imposing podium over earlier shrines.
Initially Augustan in style, at least in detail, it seems to
have been founded about the time of the death of the first
emperor and to have reached the level of the entablature
by AD 60. By the mid 3rd century AD, two monumental
altars before the temple had been enclosed by a grand
temenos flanked by colonnades with alternating rectangular
and semi-circular exedrae and preceded by an exceptional
hexagonal forecourt and triumphal propylaeum. This
was a fastigium. The curving of the entablature up
with an arch, penetrating the pediment of a temple front
between towers, recalls the twin-towered portal of the
ancient Mesopotamian palace – the place of epiphany of
god (or his representative) among men.

101 **Baalbek, Temple of Bacchus** c. AD 150, interior.
    Outside the compound, to the south, the Temple of
Bacchus was 35 by 66 metres (115 by 216 feet) with eight
by 15 columns. The cella walls, complex in plane and
exceptionally rich in articulation, enclosed a raised and
canopied sanctuary at the western end derived from the
tradition of enthroning the image of the deity in a canopied
aedicule.

102 **Palmyra, Temple of Bel** dedicated in AD 32, ceiling in southern sanctuary.

103 **Palmyra, Temple of Bel** restored view.

Dominating the prosperous trading city sited on an extensive oasis in the middle of the Syrian desert, the octostyle Temple of Bel had 15 columns on its eastern side but only 14 on its western side, where the elaborately framed entrance unconventionally intruded just to the south of the centre. A sanctuary was raised on steps and roofed at each end of the cella. Staircases in three of the four corner

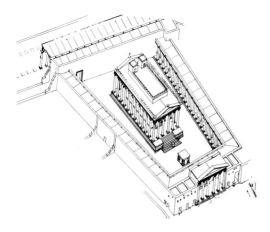

towers communicated with the terraced roof. Here the
hybrid nature of the exercise, remote from the models of
metropolitan classicism, is at its clearest: though there were
pediments at each end, merlons fringed the east and west
sides of the higher walls of the cella. By the middle of
the 2nd century AD the temenos had been enclosed by
colonnades, the western range taller than the others and
incorporating propylaea.

Mannerism

The imperial Romans far exceeded Hellenistic
builders in the prolixity with which they embellished
temple interiors.[101–102] But their interests went
beyond mere opulence.[103] They early learned to use
the Orders against the expectations induced by the
convention of the metaphor, to defy rather than to elu-
cidate structure, and anticipated the virtuoso Mannerism of the 16th century. Even at the outset of the
imperial period, the interpenetration of arch and ped-

104 **Orange, Arch of Tiberius** c. AD 21, oblique view
from the south-west.

The earliest-known work of its type to incorporate
three arches as part of the original design, it is precociously
lavish in sculptural relief as well as in the uncanonical
interpenetration of arch and Order. A consequence of
arching the entablature up into the pediment was the
removal of the arch from its natural context in the wall
altogether, recalling the arch at the eastern end of the agora
at Priene (see 23, page 58). Anticipating the fastigium of
complexes like the one at Baalbek (see 100, page 221), this was
a major imperial motif by the time of the Emperor Hadrian
(AD 117–138).

iment on the Arch of Tiberius at Orange[104] wilfully contradicts the logical articulation of the Arch of Augustus at Rimini (see 93, page 202).

The breaking of the pediment and the interpenetration of one structural form with another were to become clichés of Mannerism. Another major motif was the denial of the normal relationship between solid and void in the syncopation of the rhythm of projection and recession between storeys – running ahead a little, we shall find the outstanding antique example in the Library of Celsus at Ephesus[105] and

105 **Ephesus, Library of Celsus** c. AD 120, court front.
Incorporating the tomb of its patron (Caius Julius Celsus Polemaeanus, who had been consul) below the apse opposite the entrance, the building contained a rectangular chamber surrounded by superimposed colonnaded galleries serving three levels of bookshelves in framed recessions. The alternation of segmental and triangular pediments was a popular means of enlivening composition from late Hellenistic times. The introduction of pedestals below the bases of the columns permitted an augmentation of height without exaggerated attenuation of the proportions of the Order.

106 **Sardis, baths** 2nd century AD, view from gymnasium.

the baths and gymnasium at Sardis.[106] The wayward dislocation of load and support was anticipated in the Porta dei Borsari at Verona.[107] Here too, as at Apamea and elsewhere in the east, the spiral fluting of columns twists the conventional expression of the primitive means of dressing stone cylinders into a torsion contrary to their nature. Furthermore, on the exterior of the amphitheatre at Verona[108] the convention of articulation in terms of the familiar metaphor so clearly elucidated at the Colosseum – that the Order is the active agent, the wall passive – is mocked by the projection of the rusticated masonry to embrace, or rather devour, the pilasters.

Rococo

Mocked for their pretensions as articulating agents, twisted and displaced, the Orders and the classical repertory of ornament associated with them ultimately succumbed to stylised nature, as in the portal of the Basilica at Qanawat, where the pilasters are overwhelmed by a rampant vine.[109] This takes us

107 **Verona, Porta dei Borsari** late 1st century AD, outer face of the city gate.

ahead, to the period when the empire itself was suc-
cumbing to forces beyond its control. Before the opening of the new millennium, however, the third style of
Pompeian decoration showed the way – to the disgust
of Vitruvius – treating architecture with increasing
fantasy as a foliage-entwined filigree scenae frons
about landscapes or mythologies pictured in panels.[110] In the fourth style, developed just before the
catastrophe of AD 79, the framework overcomes all
substance or, as occasionally in the second style, the

108 **Verona, amphitheatre** late 1st century AD, detail
of perimeter.

This work is comparable with the Colosseum in structure
if not in size. At 152 by 123 metres (499 by 403 feet), it held
up to 28,000 people and the Orders of pilasters framed
only two arcades, the third level of arches rising above the
uppermost seats.

The rustication of the Order was anticipated by several
works of the Emperor Claudius (AD 41–54), most notably
the double archway carrying his new aqueducts over
converging streets, now known as the Porta Maggiore,
and the podium of the Claudianum (Temple of the Deified
Claudius).

mythologies are played out against the architecture like a theatrical entertainment.

At Qanawat, as at Pompeii, the rampant vine motif is manifestly anti-architectonic. Structure is overwhelmed by decoration, as it would be again in the rococo and art nouveau styles of the early 18th and 20th centuries. These were propagated by reformers who, like their Roman predecessors, renounced the tired tradition initiated by the Achaeans and sought the rebirth of vitality in the realm of the earth mother.

109 **Qanawat, so-called Basilica** second half of 3rd century AD, portal.

The southern Syrian town owed its prosperity to the elevation to the principate of its compatriot Philip the Arab (AD 244–49).

110 OVERLEAF **Pompeii, House of Loreius Tiburtinus, wall painting in the third style of decoration.**

glossary

ABACUS flat slab forming the top of a CAPITAL.

ACROPOLIS highest part or citadel of a city, usually the area containing the principal public buildings.

ADYTUM inner sanctum of a temple.

AEDICULE ornamental pilastered niche to house a sacred image, for example.

AEOLIC ORDER *see* ORDER, AEOLIC.

AGORA open space used as a marketplace or assembly area.

AISLE side passage of a temple, running parallel to the NAVE and separated from it by COLUMNS or PIERS.

ALA side COLONNADE of an Etruscan temple; wing to the right or left at the head of the ATRIUM of a Roman house.

AMPHITHEATRE more or less circular theatre, with banks of seats surrounding the performance space.

ANTA a PILASTER at the end of a side wall between two of which one or more COLUMNS may be placed, which are then IN ANTIS.

APADANA columned HYPOSTYLE HALL usually square in plan, with a PORTICO on one or more sides.

APODYTERIUM changing room in a Roman bath house.

APSE semi-circular domed or vaulted space, especially at one end of a BASILICA. Hence apsidal, in the shape of an apse.

AQUEDUCT artificial channel or conduit for water.

ARCADE series of arches supported by COLUMNS, sometimes paired and covered so as to form a walkway.

ARCHITRAVE one of the three principal elements of an ENTABLATURE, positioned immediately above the CAPITAL of a COLUMN, and supporting the FRIEZE and CORNICE.

ARCUATE shaped like an arch. Hence (of a building) arcuated, deploying arch structures (as opposed to TRABEATED).

ASHLAR masonry cut and placed in horizontal courses with vertical joints, so as to present a smooth surface.

ASTRAGAL small MOULDING with circular or semi-circular cross-section.

ATRIUM inner court of a Roman house, usually unroofed at the middle, where the COMPLUVIUM allowed rainwater to collect in the IMPLUVIUM.

ATTIC storey or moulded block placed immediately above the main ORDER on a building.

AXIS line used to establish geometry around which a building is designed. Hence axial plan, in which the building is related to fundamental two- or three-dimensional base lines.

BASILICA temple or other public building, consisting principally of a COLONNADED rectangular space enclosed by an ambulatory or having a central NAVE and side AISLES, often with an APSE, and generally lit by a CLERESTORY.

BEAM horizontal element in, for instance, a TRABEATED structure.

BIT-HILANI columned PORTICO, specifically of 1st millennium BC Syria.

BOULETERION meeting hall for formal gatherings of senators or councillors.

BRACKET CAPITAL load-bearing member projecting from a CAPITAL or forming a projecting CAPITAL, for instance an IONIC VOLUTE.

BUTTRESS support, usually stone, built against a wall to reinforce or take load.

CALIDARIUM hottest of the rooms in a Roman bath house.

CAPITAL top part of a COLUMN, supporting the ENTABLATURE, wider than the body of the SHAFT, usually formed and decorated more or less elaborately. The part of the COLUMN which, taken together with the ENTABLATURE, forms the major defining element in the Greek ORDERS of architecture – DORIC, IONIC and CORINTHIAN.

CAPITOL highest part or citadel of a city.

CARDO road running north to south, later the principal longitudinal road of a town or city.

CARYATID female figure used as a support in place of a COLUMN.

CATACOMB burial place, usually in the form of a passageway with recessed side galleries for the disposition of cadavers.

CAULICOLI carved plant stalks bearing the acanthus leaves supporting the VOLUTES of a CORINTHIAN CAPITAL.

CAVEA the seating within a theatre.

CAVETTO style of concave moulding with a quarter-circular cross-section.

CELLA the sanctuary of a temple, usually containing the cult statue.

CENTRING temporary wooden structure used to support an arch or VAULT under construction. (See page 182.)

CENTURATIO square measure of land.

Hence centuriation, the process of division of land into such measures.

COFFERING decoration of a ceiling or VAULT with sunken rectangular or other polygonal panels.

COLONNADE line of regularly spaced COLUMNS.

COLUMN vertical member, usually circular in cross-section, functionally structural or ornamental or both, comprising a base, SHAFT and CAPITAL.

COLUMN IN ANTIS a COLUMN deployed in a PORTICO between ANTAE as opposed to standing proud of the façade.

COMITIUM Roman assembly hall.

COMPLUVIUM rectangular opening above the centre of an ATRIUM, allowing rainwater to collect in the IMPLUVIUM.

CORBEL course of masonry or support bracket, usually stone, for a BEAM or other horizontal member. Hence corbelled, forming a stepped roof from progressively overlapping corbels.

CORINTHIAN ORDER see ORDER, CORINTHIAN.

CORNICE projecting moulding forming the top part of an ENTABLATURE.

CREPIDOMA steps forming the platform of a temple.

CRYPTOPORTICO underground passage, frequently beneath a PORTICO.

CUBICULUM bedroom of a Roman house.

CURIA Roman senate house.

CYCLOPEAN MASONRY masonry made up of massive irregular blocks of undressed stone.

DADO the middle part, between base and CORNICE, of a PEDESTAL or the lower part of a wall when treated as a continuous pedestal.

DAIS raised platform, usually at one end of an internal space.

DECASTYLE a PORTICO with ten COLUMNS.

DECUMANUS road running east to west, later the main latitudinal road of a town or city.

DENTILS small blocks deployed in horizontal lines, typically forming part of the IONIC and CORINTHIAN CORNICES.

DIPTERAL building with a double row of COLUMNS around it.

DISPLUVIATE the roof of an ATRIUM sloping upwards towards the COMPLUVIUM (as opposed to IMPLUVIATE).

DOMUS Roman town house.

DORIC ORDER *see* ORDER, DORIC.

EAVES the part of a roof which overhangs the outer face of a wall.

ECCLESIASTERION Greek assembly hall. (See pages 60–61.)

ECHINUS quarter-round convex projection or MOULDING on a cushion supporting the ABACUS of the CAPITAL of a COLUMN.

EGG-AND-DART MOULDING decoration on an OVOLO MOULDING consisting of alternating shapes of eggs and arrow-heads.

EMBRASURE an opening or indentation in a wall or PARAPET.

ENTABLATURE part of the façade immediately above the COLUMNS, usually composed of a supportive ARCHITRAVE, decorative FRIEZE and projecting CORNICE..

PISCENIA gallery on the SCENA of a theatre.

EXEDRA recess, usually APSIDAL, containing seats.

FAUCES narrow passageway giving on to an ATRIUM.

FILIGREE decorative work formed from a mesh or by piercing material to give the impression of a mesh.

FORUM central open space of a town, usually a marketplace surrounded by public buildings.

FRESCO painting done on plaster which is not yet dry.

FRIEZE the middle part of an ENTABLATURE, above the ARCHITRAVE and below the CORNICE, or more generally any horizontal strip decorated in RELIEF.

FRIGIDARIUM coolest of the rooms in a Roman bath house.

GABLE more or less triangular vertical area formed by the ends of the inclined planes of a PITCHED ROOF.

GYMNASIUM building or enclosed area for the performance of athletics.

HADITH private audience chamber in an ancient Persian royal palace.

HEXASTYLE a PORTICO with six COLUMNS.

HIGH RELIEF *see* RELIEF.

HYPOCAUST underfloor duct for heating.

HYPOSTYLE HALL hall with a roof supported by numerous COLUMNS more or less evenly spaced across its area.

IMPLUVIATE the roof of an ATRIUM sloping downwards towards the

COMPLUVIUM (as opposed to DISPLUVIATE).

IMPLUVIUM rectangular tank in the middle of the ATRIUM of a Roman house for collecting rainwater. (See page 72.)

INSULA Roman tenement or block of flats. (See pages 172–73.)

IONIC ORDER *see* ORDER, IONIC.

LAMASSU syncretic creature (winged, human-headed bull) used to guard an entrance, especially of Assyrian palaces.

LOW RELIEF: *see* RELIEF.

MEGARON rectangular hall forming the principal interior space of a palace.

MERLONS raised elements of a battlement, alternating with EMBRASURES.

MOSAIC decoration formed by embedding small coloured tiles or pieces of glass in cement.

MOULDING the contour of a projecting or inset element.

NAOS main chamber of a temple, usually housing the cult statue.

NATATIO swimming pool in a public bath house.

NAVE central body of principal interior

of, for instance, a temple.

NYMPHAEUM monumental building housing a public fountain.

OCTASTYLE a PORTICO with eight COLUMNS.

ODEON roofed building for the performance of music.

OECUS principal room of a private house.

OPISTHODOMOS porch or room at the rear of a temple, sometimes used as a treasury.

ORCHESTRA semi-circular or circular space in front of the stage of a theatre. (See pages 64–65.)

ORDER defining feature of classical architecture, comprising a COLUMN together with its ENTABLATURE.

ORDER, AEOLIC precursor of the IONIC ORDER originating in Aeolia.

ORDER, CORINTHIAN an evolution from the IONIC Order, characterised by the replacement of the CAPITAL VOLUTES with a more elaborate and deeper decorative arrangement.

ORDER, DORIC the oldest and most simply functional of the three Greek Orders of architecture, characterised by a fluted and tapered COLUMN without a base, topped by a plain

CAPITAL, surmounted by a relatively high ENTABLATURE.

ORDER, IONIC slightly later and more elaborate Order than the DORIC, featuring fluted COLUMNS that have bases and are topped by CAPITALS with scrolled VOLUTES. The COLUMNS typically are taller relative to their base diameters than the DORIC, and are correspondingly less acutely tapered. The ENTABLATURE was less tall than the DORIC, being originally composed of ARCHITRAVE and CORNICE only, though a FRIEZE became usual later.

ORTHOSTATS stone slabs deployed vertically to form the lower part of a wall.

OVOLO projecting convex MOULDING.

PALAESTRA public building for training in athletics, typically smaller than a GYMNASIUM.

PARAPET low wall, usually for defensive purposes.

PARASCENIUM projecting wings extending from the SCENA to embrace the PROSCENIUM.

PEDESTAL base supporting a COLUMN or statue.

PEDIMENT triangular area of wall, usually a gable, above the ENTABLATURE.

PERIPTERAL building whose main part is flanked by a single PERISTYLE.

PERISTYLE row of COLUMNS surrounding a building or courtyard, or a courtyard so COLONNADED.

PIER supporting pillar for a wall or roof, often of rectangular cross-section.

PILASTER a PIER of rectangular cross-section, more or less integral with and only slightly projecting from the wall which it supports.

PITCHED ROOF *see* ROOF, PITCHED.

PLINTH rectangular base or base support of a COLUMN or wall.

PODIUM continuous base or PEDESTAL, consisting of PLINTH, DADO and CORNICE, supporting a series of COLUMNS; also a platform enclosing the arena of an AMPHITHEATRE.

PORTICO entrance to a building featuring a COLONNADE.

POST vertical element in, for instance, a TRABEATED structure.

PRONAOS area in front of the principal room of a temple (the NAOS), typically with walls to the sides and COLUMNS to the fore.

PROPYLAEUM gateway, especially to a temple enclosure.

PROSCENIUM stage on which the principal actors performed, in front of the SCENA and behind the ORCHESTRA.

PROSTYLE row of COLUMNS standing in front of a building, usually forming an open PORTICO.

PROTHYRUM passage at the entrance to a building.

PTERON a COLONNADE flanking a temple.

PYRAMID structure, usually of stone, with a square base and four triangular sides meeting in a point at the top.

RELIEF carving, typically of figures, raised from a flat background by cutting away more (HIGH RELIEF) or less (LOW RELIEF) of the material from which they are carved.

REVETMENT decorative reinforced facing for a retaining wall.

ROOF, PITCHED roof composed of two inclined planes whose point of contact forms the ridge or highest line.

ROOF, TRUSSED roof supported on one or more TRUSSES.

ROSTRUM platform for public speakers (originally specific to the Forum Romanum, later more general).

ROTUNDA circular room or building, usually with a domed roof.

RUSTICATION masonry composed of blocks deeply cut at the edges relative to the centres, so as to heighten the play of light and shadow across the structure; also masonry used decoratively in its rough-cut state. (See page 234.)

SCENA structure in a theatre in front of which the principal actors performed, and behind or inside which off-stage action purported to take place.

SCENAE FRONS flat wall forming the back of the stage in a semi-circular Roman theatre.

SCOTIA concave MOULDING, usually on the base of a COLUMN, often between two convex TORUS MOULDINGS, and providing an apparently deep channel between them.

SHAFT more or less cylindrical element of a COLUMN rising from the base to the CAPITAL.

STADIUM enclosed unroofed area for the performance of athletics.

STOA extended PORTICO or roofed structure with a COLONNADE.

STUCCO type of plaster, especially used

where decoration is to be applied.

STYLOBATE top step of a CREPIDOMA, forming the base for a COLONNADE.

TABERNA small shop, workshop or (poor) dwelling opening directly on to the street.

TABLINUM principal room in a Roman house, having one side open to the ATRIUM.

TABULARIUM Roman archive building.

TEMENOS sacred enclosure, usually adjacent to a temple.

TEMPIETTO small temple.

TEMPLUM consecrated ground, marked out for the rites of augury.

TEPIDARIUM room of intermediate temperature in a Roman bath house.

TERRACOTTA baked clay used for construction or decoration of buildings or statues.

THOLOS dome, either freestanding or forming the centre of a circular building.

TORUS large convex MOULDING, typically at base of a COLUMN, of more or less semi-circular cross-section.

TRABEATED structurally dependent on rectilinear POST and BEAM supports.

TRAVERTINE light-coloured limestone.

TRICLINIUM dining room or principal reception room in a Roman house.

TRUSS timber or metal framework formed so as to support, for instance, a roof.

TRUSSED ROOF *see* ROOF, TRUSSED.

TUFA building stone of volcanic origin, more or less grey in colour.

TUMULUS ancient burial mound. (See page 104.)

TYMPANUM triangular area of a PEDIMENT enclosed by CORNICES above and ENTABLATURE below; more generally, an area, usually recessed, formed by a LINTEL below and an arch above.

VAULT structure forming an arched roof over a space. (See page 183.)

VAULT, DOMICAL enclosing a more or less hemispherical space. (See page 157.)

VAULT, BARREL enclosing a more or less hemicylindrical space.

VAULT, GROIN enclosing a space composed of two intersecting, more or less hemicylindrical,shapes.

VELARIUM awning used to shelter the audience at a Roman theatre.

VESTIBULUM entrance hall.

VILLA Roman country house.

VOLUTE scroll or spiral ornamental
  and/or support member, characteristic
  of IONIC CAPITALS.

VOUSSOIR wedge-shaped stone deployed
  in building an arch. Hence voussoir
  arch, where such stones are used.

WATTLE AND DAUB method of making
  walls using thin twigs (wattles)
  interwoven and then plastered with
  mud or clay (daub).

The books listed below are those the author found particularly useful as sources of general information on the architecture covered in this volume.

Bieber, M, *The History of the Greek and Roman Theater*, 2nd edition, Princeton 1961

Boëthius, A and Ward-Perkins, J B, *Etruscan and Roman Architecture*, London 1970

Brown, F E, *Roman Architecture*, New York 1961

Colledge, M A R, *Parthian Art*, London 1977

Curtis, J E, *Ancient Persia*, London 1989

Dennis, G, *The Cities and Cemeteries of Etruria*, 3rd edition, London 1883

Ghirshman, R, *Persia: from the origins to Alexander the Great*, London 1964

Herzfeld, E, *Iran in the Ancient East*, Oxford 1941

Lyttleton, M, *Baroque Architecture in Classical Antiquity*, London 1974

MacDonald, W L, *The Architecture of the Roman Empire, I: an introductory study*, New Haven 1965

MacDonald, W L, *The Architecture of the Roman Empire, II: an urban appraisal*, New Haven 1986

Morgan, M H, *Vitruvius. The Ten Books on Architecture*, Cambridge, Massachusetts 1914

Nash, E, *Pictorial Dictionary of Ancient Rome*, 2nd edition, 2 volumes, London 1968

Plommer, H, *Ancient and Classical Architecture (Simpson's History of Architectural Development, I)*, London 1956

IMPERIAL FORM

Richardson, E H, *The Etruscans: their Art and Civilization*,
Chicago and London 1964

Upham Pope, A, ed., *A Survey of Persian Art from Prehistoric
Times to the Present*, London and New York 1938

Ward-Perkins, J B, *Cities of Ancient Greece and Italy*,
London 1975

Ward-Perkins, J B, *Roman Architecture*, New York 1977

Wheeler, R E M, *Roman Art and Architecture*, London 1964

Sources of illustrations

page 53 W B Dinsmoor, *The Architecture of Ancient Greece*,
London 1950; pages 57, 58, 85, 216 Hugh Plommer, *Ancient and
Classical Architecture*; pages 60, 61, 79 A W Lawrence, *Greek
Architecture*, London 1973; pages 118, 138, 191, 215, 221
F E Brown, *Roman Architecture*; page 125 Leonardo Benovolo,
Storia della Città, Rome

index

maps

GAUL

Verona

DACIA

Nimes   Orange

Arles

ETRURIA

ITALY

CORSICA   LATIUM

MACEDONIA

CAMPANIA

SARDINIA

MAGNA   HELLAS

SICILY   GRAECIA

SPARTA

Carthage   Acragas

CRETE

Timgad

Lambaesis   Sbeitla   Mediterranean   Sea

NUMIDIA

Leptis Magna

Ptolemais

CYRENAICA

THE EARLY ROMAN AND ALEXANDRIAN WORLD

Black Sea

PONTUS

ANATOLIA

LYDIA

ASIA MINOR

URARTU

Caspian
Sea

NIA CARIA CILICIA

SYRIA

ASSYRIA

● Apamaea

MESOPOTAMIA

Palmyra ● ● Mari

PERSIA

● Baalbek

LEBANON ● Damascus

Babylon ●

Diocaesarea ●

Qanawat

● Susa

● Naucratis

Alexandria ●

Naqsh-i-Rustam ● Pasargadae ●

Memphis ●

● Persepolis

Saqqara ●

EGYPT

Akhetaton ●

Red
Sea

Persian
Gulf

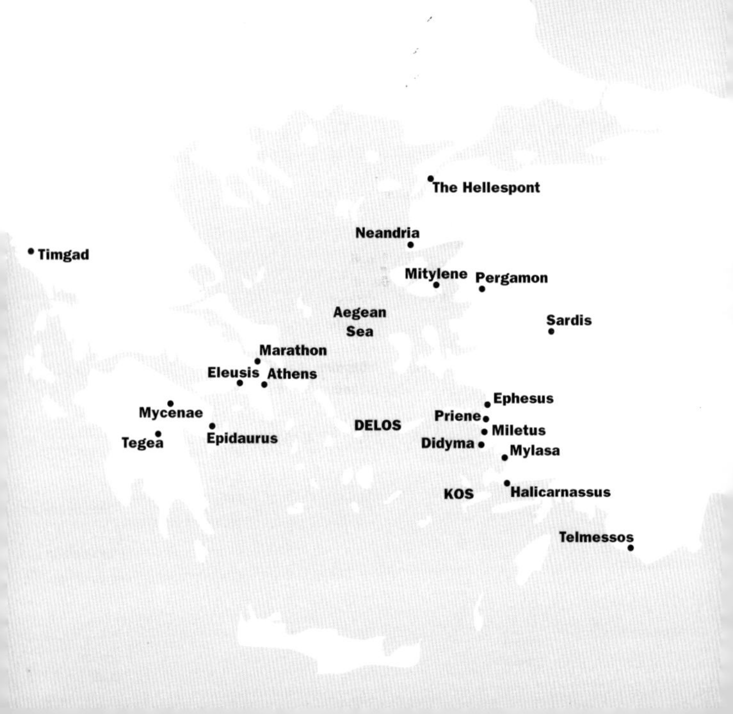

HELLENISTIC SITES

- Timgad
- The Hellespont
- Neandria
- Mitylene
- Pergamon
- Sardis

Aegean
Sea

- Marathon
- Eleusis
- Athens
- Mycenae
- Epidaurus
- Tegea
- DELOS
- Priene
- Ephesus
- Didyma
- Miletus
- Mylasa
- KOS
- Halicarnassus
- Telmessos

ITALY

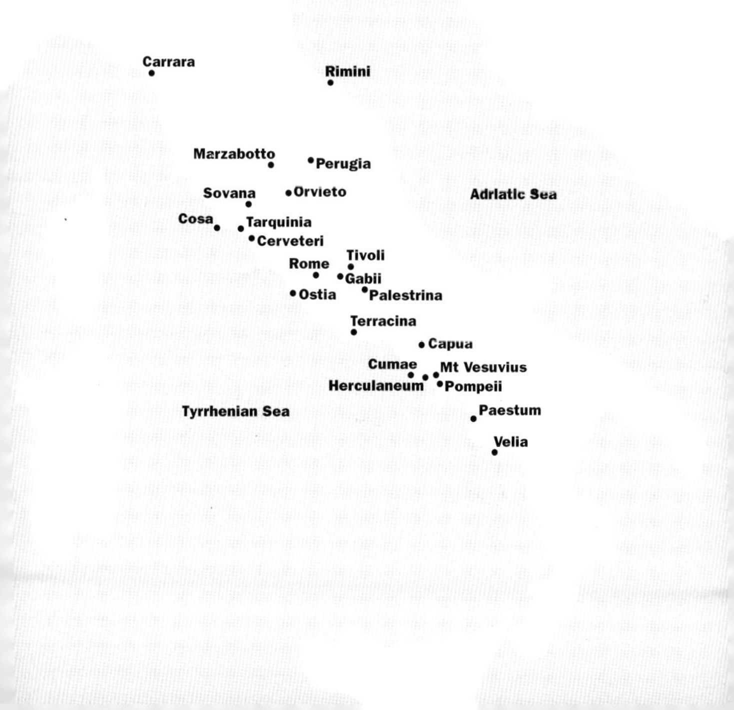

Carrara

Rimini

Marzabotto

Perugia

Sovana

Orvieto

Adriatic Sea

Cosa

Tarquinia

Cerveteri

Tivoli

Rome

Gabii

Ostia

Palestrina

Terracina

Capua

Cumae

Mt Vesuvius

Herculaneum

Pompeii

Tyrrhenian Sea

Paestum

Velia